DARK SHADOWS

RETURN TO COLLINWOOD

DARK SHADOWS

RETURN TO COLLINWOOD

KATHRYN LEIGH SCOTT
JIM PIERSON

Foreword by JONATHAN FRID

Pomegranate Press, Ltd.

NEW YORK   LOS ANGELES

© 2012 Pomegranate Press, Ltd.
First Printing 2012
Dark Shadows is a copyright of Dan Curtis Productions, Inc. & Curtis Holdings LLC.
All rights reserved.

Printed and bound in Canada

4 6 8   10 9 7 5 3

This is a Pomegranate Press, Ltd. book.
Dark Shadows: Return to Collinwood

Kathryn Leigh Scott
Jim Pierson
Foreword: Jonathan Frid
Design: Cheryl Carrington

Cover photographs courtesy Dan Curtis Productions, Inc.
Interior photographs pages 9, 10, 13, 15, 33 © Warner Bros. Inc. All Rights Reserved.
Other photos courtesy Dan Curtis Productions, Inc., Ben Martin.

Library of Congress Catalog Card Number: 2011943298
ISBN: 978-0-938817-66-6 (pbk.: alk. paper)

Pomegranate Press, Ltd.
P.O. 17217
Beverly Hills, CA 90209
FAX: (310) 271 - 4930

www.pompress.com
www.kathrynleighscott.com
pompressweb@gmail.com

Contents

Contents

Foreword
A Vampire Reflects

By

JONATHAN FRID

*I*NEVER THOUGHT WHEN *DARK SHADOWS* WENT OFF THE AIR IN APRIL OF 1971 THAT THE SERIES WOULD FIND RENEWED LIFE THROUGH RERUNS AND THROUGH THE CONTINUED INTEREST OF THE LOYAL FANS. I HAVE DONE much interesting work since but none that has reached out to so many.

Looking back at the experience of creating each half-hour episode on a daily basis, I have been astonished at the quality of the series as a whole—the many episodes which are well-written and well-played, notwithstanding the challenges the actors and the writers shared. The 1795 storyline, which revealed the origins of Barnabas, in particular stands out in my mind as *Dark Shadows* at its best—combining suspense, romance and tragedy.

I am proud to have been part of the original *Dark Shadows*, which has long provided viewing pleasure to countless people.

1968: Stuntman Alex Stevens
portrayed the werewolf.

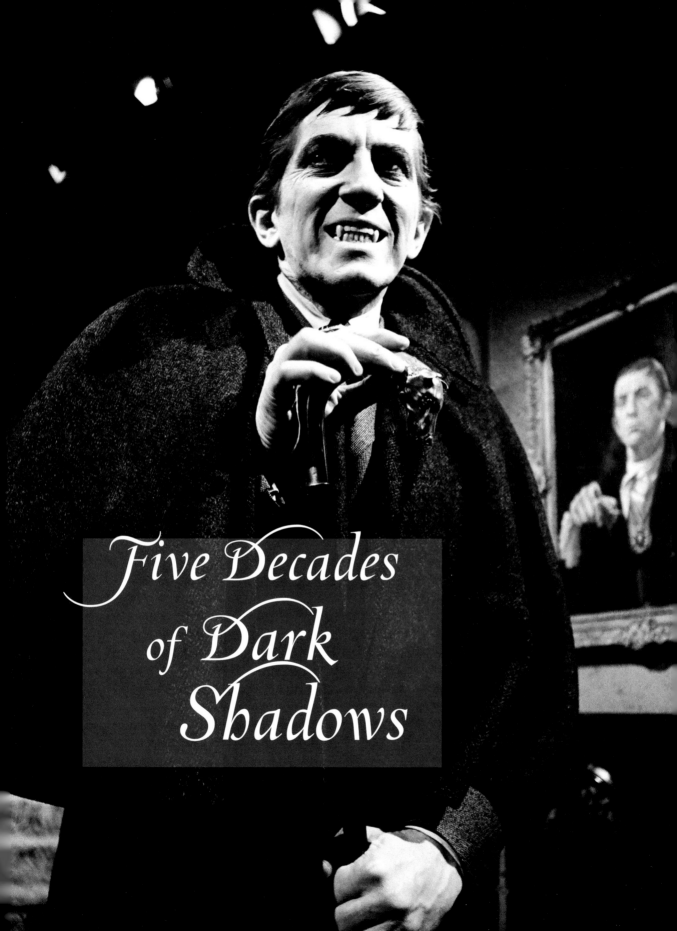

Five Decades of Dark Shadows

1966: Alexandra Motlke
as Victoria Winters.

1966

Dark Shadows debuts from Dan Curtis Productions as an ABC-TV afternoon soap opera on June 27, hailed as the first daytime drama styled in the Gothic novel tradition.

Later that year, the first of 32 Paperback Library novels penned by Dan "Marilyn" Ross and based on the series is issued, starting a *Dark Shadows* merchandising effort that will include games, gum cards and even a replica of Josette's Music Box.

1967

Jonathan Frid joins the cast as reluctant vampire Barnabas Collins and saves the series from cancellation.

1968

David Selby makes his first appearance as Quentin Collins in the form of Quentin's ghost and becomes the program's second most popular player.

Gold Key issues the first *Dark Shadows* comic book and will continue to publish them regularly until 1976.

1969

Dark Shadows achieves its highest rating with the 1897 storyline, attracting a peak of 20 million viewers in the summer of 1969.

Additionally, the *Original Music From Dark Shadows* reaches #18 on the *Billboard* album chart and the instrumental *Quentin's Theme*, covered by The Charles Randolph Grean Sound, hits #13 on the singles chart.

Jonathan Frid's *Personal Picture Album* is published by Paperback Library.

(1897 STORYLINE: DAVID SELBY AS QUENTIN COLLINS.)

1970

The MGM motion picture *House of Dark Shadows* is released in September.

Quentin's Theme is nominated for a Grammy Award as Best Instrumental.

1971

After 1,225 original episodes, *Dark Shadows* ends its ABC-TV run on April 2.

The MGM motion picture *Night of Dark Shadows* is released in August.

A *Dark Shadows* newspaper comic strip begins a one-year run nationwide.

1973

Jonathan Frid tours South America to promote Spanish language broadcasts of *Dark Shadows* which have become a huge hit in Mexico and over two dozen other countries where dubbed episodes are distributed by ABC Films and its successor, Worldvision Enterprises.

1975

Dark Shadows reruns, distributed by Worldvision, begin airing in U.S. syndication, starting with the first appearance of Barnabas' in episode 210. A total of 260 episodes are made available initially.

The World of Dark Shadows fanzine begins publishing.

1980 ShadowCon: Fans gather around original series actors John Karlen, Jerry Lacy, Michael Stroka, Lara Parker, Kathryn Leigh Scott and Humbert Allen Astredo.

1977

The first *Dark Shadows* fan convention, ShadowCon, takes place as part of Starcon in San Diego with original series actor John Karlen as guest. Stand-alone ShadowCons, devoted specifically to *Dark Shadows*, will be held in Los Angeles annually between 1979 and 1985 with many more guests and serve as a precursor to the subsequent and larger *Dark Shadows* Festivals.

The first issue of *ShadowGram*, the *Dark Shadows* current events newsletter devoted to the show and its stars, debuts.

1982

Dark Shadows reruns begin airing for the first time on a PBS station, a trend that will continue throughout the decade once the show proves to be a popular fund-raising attraction.

1983

The first *Dark Shadows* Festival is held in Newark, New Jersey, in support of the New Jersey Network of PBS stations airing reruns of *Dark Shadows*. The Festivals will continue annually, mostly alternating between the New York and Los Angeles areas, for the next three decades.

A second year of 260 episodes is released into syndication.

1985

The New Jersey Network of PBS stations airs the first *Dark Shadows Special* and begins airing a newly released third year of syndicated reruns.

1986

Pomegranate Press issues *My Scrapbook Memories of Dark Shadows* by Kathryn Leigh Scott, the first of many non-fiction, commemorative books to be issued by Scott's own independent publishing company.

1987

WYNC-TV, the city-owned PBS station in New York, airs the *Dark Shadows* special *Casting Shadows*, featuring series highlights and new interviews with cast members.

1988

Dance Theatre Workshop in New York presents an authorized stage play adaption of *Dark Shadows*, condensing the popular 1795 storyline from the original series.

1989

MPI Home Video issues the first VHS videotapes of *Dark Shadows* episodes, ultimately releasing the entire series as well as several compilations and specials in that format. Jonathan Frid appears at the Video Software Dealers Association convention in Las Vegas to promote the launch.

1991 SERIES:
BEN CROSS AS BARNABAS COLLINS

1990

The *Dark Shadows* primetime revival series begins production in March.

Quentin's Theme is awarded Broadcast Music Incorporated's one-million radio performances citation.

1991

NBC-TV airs the *Dark Shadows* primetime series for 12 episodes from January through March.

The 25th anniversary of *Dark Shadows* is celebrated with Festivals in New York and Los Angeles.

MGM Home Video releases *House of Dark Shadows* and *Night of Dark Shadows* on VHS.

1992

Reruns of the original *Dark Shadows* daytime series begins airing on the national Sci-Fi Channel cable network and will continue, except for a year break, until 2001.

1994

The Sci-Fi Channel debuts reruns of the 1991 primetime *Dark Shadows* episodes.

1999

HarperCollins publishes original series actress Lara Parker's *Angelique's Descent*, the first in a series of new *Dark Shadows* novels to be published into the 2000s when TOR Books takes over the property.

2001

The Museum of Television & Radio honors *Dark Shadows* as part of its annual Paley Television Festival on March 8 at the Director's Guild Theatre in Hollywood, where creator/executive producer Dan Curtis and over a dozen of the original series actors and production personnel reunite to discuss *Dark Shadows*.

2002

MPI Home Video begins releasing the entire original *Dark Shadows* series on DVD.

2004 PILOT:
ALEC NEWMAN AS BARNABAS.

2004

Dan Curtis Productions teams with John Wells Productions to produce a new one-hour *Dark Shadows* pilot for a prospective WB Network primetime series but the pilot does not get picked up by the network and the unfinished production is not broadcast.

Over a dozen original Dark Shadows series actors perform a new audio sequel, *Return To Collinwood*, on stage at the *Dark Shadows* Festival in Brooklyn, New York and in a Manhattan recording studio for release on CD by MPI Home Video.

2006

Dan Curtis passes away on March 27. His estate finalizes arrangements with Warner Brothers for a new *Dark Shadows* motion picture with actor Johnny Depp.

(Continued next page)

Big Finish Productions, based in England, begins releasing the first in an ongoing series of *Dark Shadows* audio drama recordings on CD featuring cast members from the original series as well as several performers from the 1991 and 2004 versions. MPI releases *Dark Shadows: The Complete Soundtrack Music Collection*, an 8-CD set containing all of the hundreds of cues composed and recorded by Robert Cobert for the original series.

2007

Jonathan Frid appears in Tarrytown, New York to celebrate the 40th anniversary of Barnabas Collins.

2010

David Selby publishes *My Shadowed Past*, a book reflecting on *Dark Shadows* as well as the social and political climate during the original series' production in the late 1960s and early 1970s.

2011

Production begins in England on the Warners Brothers motion picture of *Dark Shadows*. Original series actors Jonathan Frid, Kathryn Leigh Scott, David Selby and Lara Parker film cameo appearances.

Dynamite Comics begins publishing a new series of comic books devoted to the original *Dark Shadows*.

2012

The new *Dark Shadows* movie is scheduled for release in the United States on May 11.

Restoration on Dan Curtis' never-before-seen director's cut of *Night of Dark Shadows* is scheduled for completion and for release on DVD in 2013 along with *House of Dark Shadows*.

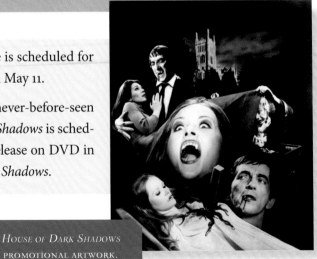

HOUSE OF DARK SHADOWS
PROMOTIONAL ARTWORK.

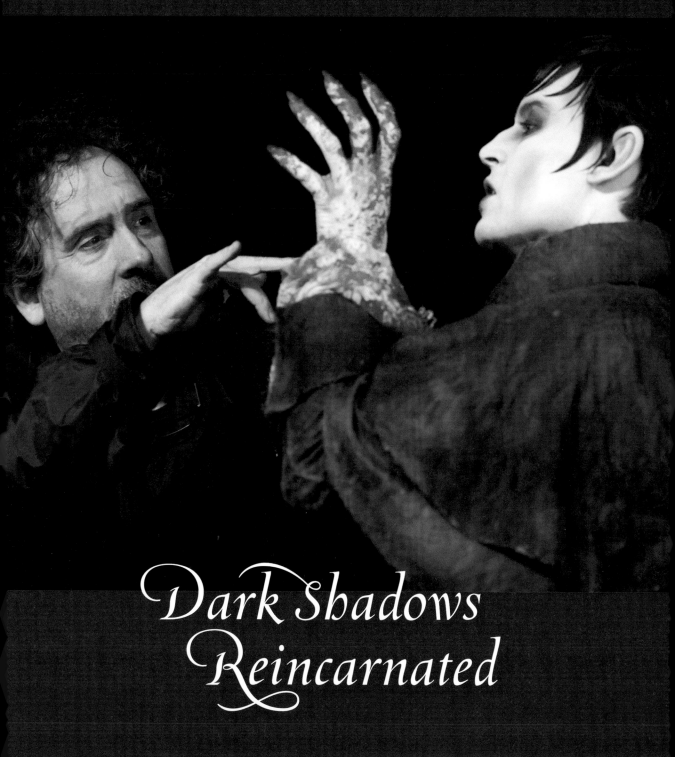

Dark Shadows
Reincarnated

2012 *Dark Shadows* movie:
David Selby, Lara Parker, Johnny Depp, Jonathan Frid,
Tim Burton and Kathryn Leigh Scott

By

JIM PIERSON

T HE 2012 *DARK SHADOWS* MOTION PICTURE REIMAGINES THE CLASSIC 1966–71 TELEVISION SERIES FEATURING TORTURED VAMPIRE BARNABAS COLLINS. ACTOR JOHNNY DEPP AND HIS LONGTIME FILMMAKING COL-league Tim Burton have taken the show they both loved from their youth and given it a fanciful, fresh spin for a new generation of viewers while also providing longtime followers with a number of surprises.

Filming of the Warner Brothers *Dark Shadows* reboot commenced on May 18, 2011 at the historic Pinewood Studios north of London. Multiple soundstages and the exterior backlot section would house an impressive array of highly-stylized sets representing the ornate and nautically appointed Collinwood mansion as well as the New England fishing village of Collinsport and its waterfront. In fact, most of the movie would be shot within the confines of Pinewood, although the Collinwood exterior set was constructed in Surrey's Bourne Woods and further locations were filmed at Beckenham Place Park, Cornwall, Crowthorne and Buckinghamshire's Black Park. The four-and-a-half month shoot concluded on September 30, 2011, a few weeks longer than anticipated due partly to the decision to feature additional visual effects. The technical feats for Burton's *Shadows* would be light years away from the pioneering Chromakey and other early forms of onscreen wizardry presented by the pre-digital 1966-1971 series and films.

Retaining the romantic elements that are at the heart of *Dark Shadows*, Depp, Burton and screenwriter Seth Grahame-Smith (author of *Abraham Lincoln: Vampire Hunter*) have chosen to accentuate the bizarre aspects of the wealthy and privileged Collins family, infusing the film with humor and poignancy as

DARK SHADOWS 1967 TELEVISION CAST, LEFT TO RIGHT:
DAVID HENESY (DAVID COLLINS), KATHRYN LEIGH SCOTT (MAGGIE EVANS),
SHARON SMYTH (THE GHOST OF SARAH COLLINS), ANTHONY GEORGE (BURKE DEVLIN),
ROBERT GERRINGER (DR. DAVID WOODARD), DENNIS PATRICK (JASON MCGUIRE),
NANCY BARRETT (CAROLYN STODDARD), JOHN KARLEN (WILLIE LOOMIS),
ALEXANDRA MOLTKE (VICTORIA WINTERS), JONATHAN FRID (BARNABAS COLLINS),
GRAYSON HALL (DR. JULIA HOFFMAN), CLARICE BLACKBURN (MRS. JOHNSON),
DANA ELCAR (SHERIFF GEORGE PATTERSON), LOUIS EDMONDS (ROGER COLLINS)
AND JOAN BENNETT (ELIZABETH COLLINS STODDARD).

Dark Shadows 2012 movie cast, left to right:
Helena Bonham Carter (Dr. Julia Hoffman), Chloe Moritz (Carolyn Stoddard),
Eva Green (Angelique), Gulliver McGrath (David Collins), Bella Heathcote
(Victoria Winters), Johnny Depp (Barnabas Collins), Ray Shirley (Mrs. Johnson),
Jackie Earle Haley (Willie Loomis), Jonny Lee Miller (Roger Collins)
and Michelle Pfeiffer (Elizabeth Collins Stoddard).

vampire Barnabas Collins breaks free from his bonds and returns to the modern world of Collinwood two centuries after he was locked away as a cursed creature of the night.

Johnny Depp has recalled, "I do remember, very vividly, practically sprinting home from school in the afternoon to see Jonathan Frid play Barnabas Collins. Even then, at that age, I knew—this has got to be weird. Over the years, these vampire movies have come out . . . vampire TV shows and stuff like that, and you go, 'Well, nobody looks like a vampire, man. What happened?' I adored *Dracula*, still do, from Bela Lugosi to Christopher Lee. It was an opportunity to sort of go into something that doesn't exist so much anymore, which is classic monster makeup and a classic monster character." As an homage, Depp has embraced not only the famous Barnabas bangs in his hairstyle and the traditional wolf's head cane but also requested customized ear prosthetics to closely resemble Frid's appearance as Barnabas.

Depp adds, "Ironically, you know, Tim had gone through the same experience. We were doing *Sweeney Todd* a couple of years ago . . . One day, we're just sitting there talking and I said 'You know, we should do a vampire movie sometime. Let's do a vampire movie.' I went, "Oh, *Dark Shadows*, man,' . . . and then one thing led to another."

"In some sense he can be a terrifying killer; on the other hand, women have a weakness for him and he has a weakness for women," Seth Grahame-Smith says. "He can be a very well-mannered, well-meaning vampire most of the time, until his stomach is empty or someone challenges his beloved Collins family."

As portrayed by Johnny Depp, Barnabas Collins is the undead equivalent of a "fish out of water," learning to adapt in a contemporary world where his descendants have fallen upon hard times. The members of the Collins family—including matriarch Elizabeth Collins Stoddard (Michelle Pfeiffer), her teenaged daughter Carolyn (Chloe Moretz), Elizabeth's brother Roger (Jonny Lee Miller) and his young son David (Gulliver McGrath) are all considerably more quirky than in previous *Dark Shadows* productions, a description that applies to most elements in the 2012 motion picture.

While certain familiar plot points remain at the foundation of the latest incarnation of *Dark Shadows*, the Depp/Burton/Grahame-Smith team takes the original tale into unexpected realms while attempting to honor the spirit of late

DARK SHADOWS 2012:
MICHELLE PFEIFFER, TIM BURTON
AND JONNY LEE MILLER.

series creator Dan Curtis, to whom the 2012 film is dedicated. The story is now centered in 1972—the year after the original series ended production, allowing a setting far removed from the time of Barnabas' origin and a period rich with hippies, rock music and materialistically-driven melodrama.

CAST OF CHARACTERS

BARNABAS COLLINS (JOHNNY DEPP)—Born in the 1740s, Barnabas relocates from England to America with his parents and finds himself in charge of the family's shipping business. A romantic fling with a vengeful witch named Angelique casts darkness on Barnabas and the Collins family. He is cursed as a vampire and confined to a coffin for two centuries, until his unplanned release in 1972.

VICTORIA WINTERS (BELLA HEATHCOTE)—Hired to become the governess of disturbed young David Collins, Victoria Winters comes to Collinwood and is immediately drawn into an intriguing and intimate relationship with another newcomer, Barnabas Collins. Victoria also possesses a mysterious past, one that seemingly connects her to Barnabas once he feels she is the reincarnation of his lost love Josette DuPres from the 1700s.

ANGELIQUE BOUCHARD (EVA GREEN)—Having met and loved Barnabas during his youth in the 1700s, Angelique cursed him as a vampire when he ended their affair. Angelique has continued to seek revenge against the Collins family with a competing cannery. When she discovers that Barnabas is free from his 200-year incarceration, Angelique unleashes her strongest supernatural fury to finally destroy him and the entire Collins clan.

ELIZABETH COLLINS STODDARD (MICHELLE PFEIFFER)—The Collins matriarch, Elizabeth Collins Stoddard is a reclusive, slightly off-center woman with dark secrets. She is the mother of teenager Carolyn Stoddard and also looks after David, the son of Elizabeth's self-centered brother Roger. Although the family is in financial and personal turmoil, Elizabeth finds a new ally when Barnabas Collins introduces himself.

ROGER COLLINS (JONNY LEE MILLER)—The greedy and abusive head of the Collins business enterprises, Roger Collins is Elizabeth's younger brother. He has squandered the family's money and focuses entirely on his own self-interests. His efforts to project himself otherwise are as pathetic as his neglectful care of his troubled but precocious son David.

DR. JULIA HOFFMAN (HELENA BONHAM CARTER)—A hard-drinking psychiatrist, Dr. Hoffman lives at Collinwood where she has futilely attempted to help young David Collins deal with his perceived demons. With the arrival of Barnabas, Julia finds herself a new subject of interest and someone that interests her beyond professional pursuits.

CAROLYN STODDARD (CHLOË MORETZ)—The rebellious, music-loving teenage daughter of Elizabeth, Carolyn suffers from the isolated existence of the Collins family. She prefers privacy over the companionship of her oddball family but welcomes the presence of new member Barnabas Collins, with whom she shares something in common.

DAVID COLLINS (GULLIVER MCGRATH)—Another victim of the strange, surreal lifestyle of the Collins family, the disturbed young David Collins is a child with an irresponsible and indifferent father, Roger. Additionally, David insists upon having contact with his deceased mother as well as other commuication with the hereafter.

WILLIE LOOMIS (JACKIE EARLE HALEY)—The quintessential burned-out bum, Willie Loomis is Collinwood's resident handyman, although his usefulness has been compromised by too much alcohol and too little care. However, his life takes an extreme turn once Barnabas appears.

MRS. JOHNSON (RAY SHIRLEY)—The elderly, decrepit housekeeper has been a servant at Collinwood for decades. However, whatever secrets she has witnessed are seemingly kept to herself as she has lost her hearing and is nearly blind.

DARK SHADOWS (2012) MOTION PICTURE SYNOPSIS

In the year 1752, Joshua and Naomi Collins, with young son Barnabas, set sail from Liverpool, England to start a new life in America. But even an ocean is not enough to escape the mysterious curse that has plagued their family. Two decades pass and Barnabas has the world at his feet—or at least the town of Collinsport, Maine. Barnabas, the master of Collinwood Manor, is rich, powerful and an inveterate playboy—until he makes the grave mistake of breaking the heart of Angelique Bouchard. A witch in every sense of the word, Angelique dooms him to a fate worse than death: turning him into a vampire, and then burying him alive. Two centuries later, Barnabas is inadvertently freed from his tomb and emerges into the very changed world of 1972. He returns to Collinwood Manor to find that his once-grand estate has fallen into ruin. The dysfunctional remnants of the Collins family have fared little better, each harboring their own dark secrets. Matriarch Elizabeth Collins Stoddard has called upon live-in psychiatrist, Dr. Julia Hoffman, to help with her family troubles. Also residing in the manor is Elizabeth's ne'er-do-well brother, Roger Collins; her rebellious teenage daughter Carolyn Stoddard; and Roger's precocious 10-year-old son, David Collins. The mystery extends beyond the family, to caretaker Willie Loomis and David's new nanny, Victoria Winters.

Journey Back to Collinwood

By

Kathryn Leigh Scott

"Jonathan is in! He'll do it! You'll all be on set in Pinewood shooting Friday, July first." Jim Pierson sounded triumphant, as well he should.

As the longtime promotional and marketing director for *Dark Shadows* with Dan Curtis Productions and the Dan Curtis estate, Jim was serving as a consultant on the film and had worked quietly behind the scenes to coordinate our cameo appearances in the new Warner Bros. film. His jubilant phone call made it official.

Jonathan Frid, who created the role of vampire Barnabas Collins in the original ABC-TV afternoon soap and starred in the first MGM film based on the show (*House of Dark Shadows*), had agreed to fly from his native Canada to England to play a cameo in the new feature starring Johnny Depp. *Dark Shadows*, directed by Tim Burton, had already been in production for five weeks at England's Pinewood Studios in Iver Heath, Buckinghamshire. David Selby (Quentin Collins), Lara Parker (Angelique Bouchard) and I (Josette DuPrés) were also on board to appear in the film.

Altogether, it was a dream come true for legions of fans loyal to the afternoon soap that millions of kids "ran home from school to watch," longing to see some of their favorite actors appear in the new film. It was also a gratifying gesture to a core group of original cast members who had launched their careers on *Dark Shadows* some 45 years earlier. In the late 1960s, David, Lara and I were "the kids" on the show, newcomers to television who were lucky enough to work with such distinguished veteran actors as Academy Award nominee Grayson Hall

(Dr. Julia Hoffman), Thayer David (Count Petofi), Louis Edmonds (Roger Collins) and Hollywood screen legend Joan Bennett (Elizabeth Collins), among others.

Canadian actor Jonathan Frid, who had graduated from England's Royal Academy of Dramatic Arts in 1945, was 87 years old. He was still game to perform, and enjoyed presenting dramatic readings occasionally. But his hearing was poor. He tired easily. Barnabas' signature prop, the silver wolf's-head cane now served him as a walking stick. And, despite voicing his eagerness to appear in the new film, it was clear traveling from his residence in a small town some distance from Toronto to London, followed by a long drive to a hotel in Northamptonshire, England, would be an arduous journey. Handling luggage, immigration and customs alone would be daunting for an elderly man after a ten-hour flight. To seal the deal, Jim Pierson arranged to fly to Canada and escort Jonathan on the journey to England.

David, Lara and I would fly from Los Angeles to London. However, even our scheduling wasn't easy. David Selby was tied up with another project on Monday evening and couldn't leave until Tuesday. Lara Parker's passport had expired. She had to apply for an emergency passport, which she hoped to have in hand by the following Monday. Meanwhile, anticipation mounted as travel arrangements were made and we checked out online photographs of The Grove, a luxury estate and spa some distance from Pinewood Studios, where we would be staying.

"So next Tuesday's our travel day," Jim said. "We'll all meet up at the hotel in England on Wednesday and go to Pinewood for wardrobe fittings."

"I'm packed and ready to go now," I said. "Please get me on a flight to London tomorrow!"

"Don't know if I can," he laughed. "How about Sunday?"

I left Sunday, June 26th, on a Virgin Atlantic flight to London, giving me a few extra days to visit friends, see some theatre and wrestle through dreaded bouts of jet lag before I was scheduled to be at the studio on Wednesday. Even as I boarded the late afternoon flight, I couldn't quite believe that Jonathan, Lara, David and I would actually all be working together again some 40 years after the original series went off the air. Ever since the first rumors had swirled four years earlier that Johnny Depp's production company had optioned the property from the Dan Curtis Estate, several of us from the original casts of both the 1966–71 series and the 1970–71 feature films (*House of Dark Shadows* and *Night of Dark Shadows*) had harbored hopes of playing cameo roles in the new Warner Bros. production. I was certainly one of those most eager for a chance to take part in the latest incarnation.

In 1990, when I arrived on location in Vancouver, B.C., to guest-star in an episode of the television series that made Johnny Depp a star, *21 Jump Street,* the first words I heard upon entering the makeup trailer were, "*Dark Shadows* is Johnny Depp's favorite show—someday he'd love to play Barnabas Collins!" As it happened, I had no scenes with Johnny in that episode and no opportunity to meet and talk with him about his interest in *Dark Shadows*. For the next several years, as Depp created one unique film character after another, I couldn't imagine any other actor playing the role Jonathan Frid had originated. In Edward Scissorhands, Ed Wood, J. M. Barry and Jack Sparrow, one could see the creative juices on tap for his own characterization of the iconic vampire Barnabas Collins.

The first inkling that Johnny Depp might actually take on the role of Barnabas came in 2006, the year that *Dark Shadows* creator Dan Curtis died. In July it was reported that Warner Bros. was teaming with Johnny Depp's Infinitum-Nihil and Graham King's GK Films to develop a feature based on the '60s supernatural TV show *Dark Shadows*. Waves of unconfirmed reports followed that Tim Burton, who was at work on *Alice in Wonderland*, had his eyes set on directing a revamp of *Dark Shadows*. Johnny Depp was revealed to be involved not only as a producer but actually starring as Barnabas, and screenwriter John August was said to be

BACK: DAVID KENNEDY, MARIE WALLACE, JOHN KARLEN, DAVID SELBY, JIM PIERSON. FRONT: KATHRYN LEIGH SCOTT, JONATHAN FRID, LARA PARKER

already at work on a script. Burton, Depp and August had previously collaborated on both *Charlie and the Chocolate Factory* and *The Corpse Bride*. It sounded like a winning combination for *Dark Shadows* and enticing enough for me to put "Dark Shadows" on permanent Google alert.

In early December 2008, producer Richard Zanuck revealed that, "*Dark Shadows* is going to be Tim's next project after *Alice in Wonderland* and they'll be shooting it next summer in London." In the Spring, the remake had still not been given a green light, and John August was reportedly working on rewrites for a possible autumn start date.

That summer, Jonathan Frid, who had not attended a *Dark Shadows* Festival (fan convention/cast reunion) since the early 1990s until returning in 2007, decided to join us for our 2008 three-day event in mid-August to be held in Burbank, California. To celebrate Jonathan's special visit, I organized a small dinner party at my house with several of the original actors. I then suggested to Jim Pierson and David Kennedy, who was attached as a producer on the film, that Johnny Depp, Tim Burton and John August might want to join us for dinner. It was a fanciful notion, but then if this amazing trio wanted to remake *Dark Shadows*, an intimate gathering with members of the original cast might strike them as a golden opportunity to refresh their memories of the show and the roles we played. For several tantalizing weeks, the possibility lingered that one or more of them might actually show up. In the end, Jonathan, Lara, David, Marie Wallace ("Jenny Collins"), John Karlen ("Willie Loomis") and I, along with Jim Pierson and David Kennedy, enjoyed dinner in my garden without the dazzling "surprise guests" joining us.

Rumors about possible start dates ebbed and flowed while Tim Burton worked longer than expected on post-production for *Alice in Wonderland* and Johnny Depp committed to filming *The Tourist* with Angelina Jolie as well as another installment of *Pirates of the Caribbean*. Finally, in December 2009, producer Graham King predicted that *Dark Shadows* would begin shooting with Depp and Burton around September or October of 2010.

In July 2010, Seth Grahame-Smith, who had written novels that put a macabre twist on literary classics (*Pride and Prejudice and Zombies*) and historical figures (*Abraham Lincoln Vampire Hunter*), was hired to write a new draft of *Dark Shadows*. The film had been pushed back once more and was now slated to begin production in early 2011. Shooting was postponed again, but in December of 2010,

L TO R: DAVID SELBY, LARA PARKER, JONATHAN FRID, KATHRYN LEIGH SCOTT, JOHN KARLEN, MARIE WALLACE.

a copy of the script fell into my hands courtesy of a London theatrical agent. I read it and lo and behold, I liked it! It was fun, fanciful, tongue-in-cheek without being campy and—most appealing to me—had an original storyline with an intriguing Rip Van Winkle twist. The new version did not expand on any of the various *Dark Shadows* plots from the original series or the previous two feature films, nor did it bear any resemblance to the short-lived primetime NBC-TV adaptation from 1991 or the 2004 WB Network pilot.

Also, the film was set in 1972, the year after the original *Dark Shadows* went off the air. According to screenwriter Seth Grahame-Smith, "Tim and Johnny took a long time explaining exactly why it had to be 1972. 1969 was too early and 1973 was too late. 1972 is right at the time when the hippie movement and all its peace and love is dying out and being replaced by this me-me-me generation in the '70s who are all about showing their wealth and having everything."

I cautiously shared the bootleg script with a few cohorts. None of us saw likely roles for ourselves, unless we all stood in as Collinwood "city council-members." Could Jonathan pass as an "ancient fisherman?" Would Lara and I be cast as "village spinsters?" Who could David Selby play? By the time we arrived in London, we had some idea of the scenes in which we were to appear, but we hadn't been given a shooting script. None of us had ever done "extra work"—and we all had concerns about being shuffled into a crowd scene. Would we have any dialogue? And exactly what constituted a cameo? Tim Burton and Johnny Depp had been quoted often about their devotion to the show and its original cast members—we trusted they wouldn't allow us to look foolish.

In an interview with MTV on February 14, 2010, Johnny delivered what amounted to a valentine to Jonathan: "What Jonathan Frid did with that character and that classic look he created, I find it very difficult to stray very far from that . . . I think it's going to be somewhere in that area, with maybe just a couple of different touches here and there . . . There's something about this vampire coming back after 200 years into this modern world, with a touch of the poetic . . . I have a good feeling about it. But Jonathan Frid's Barnabas was so special."

Indeed. We arrived in London with every reason to trust.

A studio car delivered me to Pinewood at 11 a.m. Wednesday, June 29th. I'd worked at the studio many times over the years, the first occasion in 1973 when I filmed the role of Catherine in *The Great Gatsby*. This time, on a cloudless sunny day, we drove up to the entry gates past a mammoth half-built, raw wood structure that soon would be used as a set for one of two upcoming remakes of *Snow White*.

I was shown to my dressing room, then immediately taken to the wardrobe studio, where Lara Parker was already being fitted for her costume. On the way, I ran into David Selby choosing among various styles of "mutton chops" in the makeup room. We had a hurried conference concerning Jonathan. Jim Pierson had just called me on my cell phone to say that Jonathan, after some 20 hours of travel, was tired and disoriented. He'd been delayed going through customs and immigration, and had had little sleep since his arrival. Our "reluctant vampire" was already worn out and anxious to go home. Jim, too, was anxious because Jonathan was quite insistent about catching the next flight back to Toronto. I assured Jim that if he could get Jonathan to Pinewood, I would forewarn the wardrobe supervisor that our dear friend required some special handling.

I'd been eager to meet Colleen Atwood, the award-winning costume designer on many of Tim Burton's films, including *Edward Scissorhands* and *Legend of Sleepy Hollow*. I'd recently seen some of her drawings and costumes on display at the Los Angeles County Museum of Art (LACMA) Tim Burton exhibit. However, almost my first words upon seeing her were, "Jonathan's a little under the weather after his long trip. Is it possible to fit him somewhere downstairs closer to the entrance?" I realized I'd made Jonathan sound like a prima donna, and immediately added, "It's a little hard for him to walk. He's 87-years-old."

"He is?" Colleen gave me a questioning look and then said, "I had no idea. We'll take care of it."

I then began trying on the first of eight long gowns, all of them in various shades of plum and claret, except for the last. It was black, slim-fitting and high-necked with long chiffon sleeves and patterns of tiny gold beads. I loved it. We then selected accessories, including a stunning gold necklace and earrings. I was taken for brief stops to meet the heads of makeup and hairdressing, and then Lara, David and I joined Jim Pierson and Jonathan Frid in a downstairs fitting area. Lara and David had arrived in England only that morning and been driven straight from Heathrow airport to Pinewood. Both were exhausted. But it was Jonathan who clearly showed the stress and fatigue of his long journey. Lara and I gave him hugs and fussed over him, which seemed to buoy him up. David, with his congenial good humor, was also a tonic. Richard Zanuck arrived to welcome us, and I photographed him with Jonathan as we all stood talking with the legendary producer.

Then, while Jim, Lara, David and I hovered, chatting and cajoling, Jonathan tried on velvet evening jackets and dress shirts. All I could think was, *plus ça change*. We've all gone our separate ways over the past forty years, but when we get together it's as though no time at all has passed. We immediately revert to our old familiar bonds. We were in this together and we weren't going to let our side down. We'd be looking out for each other, and especially our most senior member. Jonathan rallied with all the attention and seemed delighted by the tour we were taken on by beautiful, smiling Sarah Clark, the unit publicist.

Our first stop was the production office. From the moment we arrived at Pinewood, we'd wielded our cameras with abandon, photographing each other and everything that caught our attention in the makeup, hairdressing and wardrobe rooms. In the art department, the walls were covered with drawings and

RICHARD ZANUCK AND JONATHAN FRID

photographs of the sets. We photographed everything in sight. All that came to an abrupt halt when Sarah handed around confidentiality agreements for us to sign and told us that we were not permitted to use our cameras. Try telling a child not to stick a hand in an open cookie jar! The temptation was particularly over-powering when we were told we'd be visiting the Collinwood set, but we dutifully pocketed our cameras as we walked through the heavy padded doors.

For an actor, walking onto a dank, chilled sound stage, with its smells of dust, paint resin, hot lights and humanity, is virtually the same the world over. One steps over cables and heads with purpose toward the circle of light, ready to work. But I found walking onto the set of *Dark Shadows* that day to be an entirely different experience. I felt oddly like a tourist, and wondered if the others had similar feelings. I wanted to walk on set as an actor, but I felt more like a novelty. It occurred to me how many times over the years I had finished a scene and then been ushered over to meet "guests-to-the-set," distinguished VIPs or someone's out-of-town family members. That's *not* who I wanted to be—nor did I want to be "omigosh, I used to run home from school to watch you!" Not that day, not on *that* set.

Miraculously, those churlish thoughts vanished as two figures emerged from the gloom of the darkened drawing room set: Tim Burton and Johnny Depp.

Jonathan Frid viewing set designs in Pinewood production office

Burton, big and bear-like, smiled and grasped my hand. "So glad you're with us," he said. The words "with us" made all the difference in the world. I could have hugged him.

Then I heard, "We've so been looking forward to having you join us." I don't know who spoke those words, but I could guess. Any lingering thoughts of feeling like a tourist traveling from another century vanished.

Johnny Depp, bone-thin in Barnabas costume and makeup, held out his hand. He was gracious and warm—and entirely in character. Had he really been consuming green tea to slim down, as had been reported in various online blogs? There wasn't a glimmer of Jack Sparrow or Ed Wood. He was Barnabas Collins, his silver wolf's-head cane in hand.

Standing next to me, leaning on his own silver wolfs-head cane, was the other Barnabas. I seized my opportunity to tell Johnny Depp how much all the *Dark Shadows* actors appreciated his generous remarks about Jonathan. Burton and Depp both looked at Jonathan and said, "But we wouldn't be here without you."

Jonathan smiled and nodded, looking very pleased as he closely analyzed his successor's appearance. "Your hair," he said, looking at Depp. "I see you've done the hair." After another moment of scrutiny, he added, "But a few more spikes."

With a whisper of a smile, Johnny murmured, "We're doing things a little differently."

Sarah organized a group photo, and we all stood with our arms around each other. Minutes later we were on our way to a van, our luggage already piled high in the back, that would take us to the luxurious Grove Hotel and Spa in the rolling English countryside. Jonathan, who had checked in after arriving in the middle of the night, was impatient and tired. "This drive back again!" he said, looking out the window. "Endless."

"But wonderful scenery," Lara said.

"Hmmmph," Jonathan said. "I can see the same at home."

"Let's meet up for drinks at the hotel," I suggested.

"Well, now you're talking!" Jonathan said, and we all laughed.

The Grove Hotel, formerly a stately home, was set in several acres of manicured lawns, with golf and tennis courts. My room looked out on the charming flower and vegetable gardens. I quickly unpacked and decided I'd figure out how to work the state-of-the-art flat screen "entertainment center" another time—or not. I met up with Lara and we joined David, Jim and Jonathan in the bar.

"What do you think they thought of us?" Lara asked. Then I knew we'd probably shared the same feelings on the set.

"Old fogeys, that's what!" David laughed. "But they were nice."

"But what are we supposed to *be*?" Jonathan rumbled. "What's the scene? What do we say? There's no script!" He thumped his cane on the floor. "We can't just stand there like ninnies!" The word "ninnies" was so explosive, we laughed—then quickly reassured Jonathan we all agreed with him.

"Jim, I want to see a script or I'm going home," he said ominously. "That's it. Home."

Jim, who often bore the brunt of Jonathan's displeasure, looked unhappy. "No one has a scene breakdown," he said. "I haven't seen one."

I jumped in. "They wouldn't have brought us all here if they didn't have a nice scene in mind."

Jonathan gave me a look. "Hmmmph, you're just saying that."

He was right, of course. I said it because I wanted it to be true. I also wanted to make the most of this unlikely experience. "How about another round," I said, catching the waiter's eye.

"And some food," David added.

2011: AT THE HOTEL IN ENGLAND DURING FILMING OF THE *DARK SHADOWS* MOVIE: LARA PARKER, KATHRYN LEIGH SCOTT, DAVID SELBY, JIM PIERSON AND JONATHAN FRID.

"I'll tell you what I think," I said. "I think they've already figured out that we're a handful. Anyway, I like my gown."

"So do I," Lara said, "and that's all that matters!" We both started laughing because, in a way, it was true, too.

We spent most of the following day at Pinewood touring the back lot where the exterior Collinsport sets had been constructed. I gaped in amazement as we walked up an asphalt ramp and looked across at a harbor scene complete with sailing ships and fishing boats bobbing in the water. The Collinsport Cannery, a vast timber building, half in ruins, stood adjacent to the docks. Across from it, Angel Bay, a two-story red-painted cannery was still under construction. It was an eerie experience to walk the cobblestone streets and peer around at an old-fashioned filling station, quaint cottages and shop fronts and see the mythical town of Collinsport come alive much as I somehow imagined it.

But then I'd walked the narrow streets of the old waterfront area of Newport, Rhode Island, with its converted harbor shops where the longships had been built, that had inspired the sets for the *Dark Shadows* series. Maggie Evans, the Collinsport Diner waitress I played in the opening episodes, had lived in a rough-hewn cottage near the harbor, where her father, Sam Evans, painted seascapes to please the tourist crowd. I'd also dined at The Black Pearl restaurant, a low-slung shanty that had served as the prototype for The Blue Whale, where I'd played many scenes with Mitch Ryan (Burke Devlin) and my boyfriend, Joe Haskell (Joel Crothers). I felt right at home.

We also toured the interior Collinwood foyer and great hall set that took up an entire soundstage. Our small television studio on New York's West 53rd street had regularly housed the permanent Collinwood sets, as well as The Old House, Blue Whale, Maggie's Collinsport Diner set and whatever patches of rock and greens stood in for gloomy exterior shots. The Collinwood set at Pinewood featured broad stairs that could have been used for a Busby Berkeley dance number, yet the fireplace, stained-glass windows and wood-paneled walls hung with family portraits were reminiscent of the sets we'd once used in the series. In the drawing room set, David and Jonathan stood for long minutes gazing up at an oil painting of Barnabas Collins, while I looked around for my Josette portrait.

Sarah Clarke then took us for a late lunch in the Pinewood Executive Dining Room. Before we'd even ordered, it was apparent that jet lag was taking its toll on Jonathan. Jim ushered him to his dressing room where he could nap while the rest

Jonathan Frid, Johnny Depp, Kathryn Leigh Scott, Lara Parker, Tim Burton, David Selby and Jonny Lee Miller on set of 2012 *Dark Shadows*.

Behind the scenes of the 2012 movie: Jonathan Frid with (costume designer) Colleen Atwood, David Selby.

of us finished dining. By late afternoon, we were back at The Grove making plans to meet for drinks and a light dinner.

That night I went to bed early, hoping to get a good night's sleep before my 5 a.m. wakeup call. A car would be picking up Lara and me at 6 a.m. for the half-hour drive to Pinewood. We'd been scheduled for the first setup of the day, largely in deference to Jonathan, who woke early and tired as the day wore on. In truth, the early start suited all of us. Somewhere in a distant part of the hotel, a band was playing. I lay in bed, listening to the faint music, thinking about our ballroom scene the following morning. What would Maggie Evans make of all this? To streamline the story in the new film version, Victoria Winters, the original governess played by Alexandra Moltke, becomes Josette DuPrés. But in the series, it was Maggie who became Josette, the doomed love interest of Barnabas Collins. And it was as Maggie Evans that I'd been invited to the ball.

I'd long imagined that Maggie Evans, who'd been carted off for treatment at the Windcliff sanitarium following her nervous breakdown, was cured by a young, brilliant, very handsome neurologist, who fell in love with her. Once she left the clinic, the doctor courted her and they married, children to follow. A boy and girl, of course. Names? I'd settled on Jack and Nell. They lived happily in a great, sprawling house on a hill overlooking waves crashing on a rocky shore. For Maggie, the motherless child, who had been raised by her drunken, penniless father, it was a dream life that would only get better. Maggie, with her vivid imagination and gift for storytelling, would become a world-renowned, best-selling author of cozy mysteries. Alas, her husband dies, ironically of a brain aneurism. Maggie, an empty-nester, whose adorable children were leading purposeful lives in distant places, turned her lovely vast home into a Bread & Breakfast, where she frequently hosted writing seminars. The girl who'd grown up on the wrong side of the tracks was now a distinguished member of the community—so, of course, she'd been invited to attend the ball given by the newly-arrived Barnabas Collins in the old Collinwood mansion.

Question: Would there be that magical moment when the now-matronly (yes, let's face it!) Maggie Evans would lock eyes with the charismatic paramour of her youth—indeed, Barnabas Collins!—the very man who had brought her to the edge of insanity?

I doubted it. Besides, in the film's 1972 setting, how to account for the forty-plus intervening years—unless, of course, the new *Dark Shadows* film was one long dream sequence. My mind swirled and I drifted off to sleep, knowing that I would not be mentioning any of these random thoughts to Mr. Burton the following day. But at least I had some backstory that accounted for my elegant gown and fancy hairdo—and my invitation to the Collinwood Ball.

Two sleepy middle-aged women with damp hair and no makeup climbed into a waiting car the following morning and grinned like schoolgirls. By 6:45 a.m. Lara and I were seated side-by-side in makeup chairs. It was clear from the beginning that the two expert makeup artists assigned to us had taken "1972" seriously. Tacked to the mirrors were vintage fashion pictures of women with froths of frozen hair and glittery turquoise eye shadow. My heart sank as glittery turquoise eye shadow was brushed onto my own eyelids. Oh, no, this would not do. It was a stylish look for a hip, young party-goer of the time, but on me it was garish and inappropriate—Maggie Evans, esteemed author and venerable community leader, could not arrive at the ball looking like Mae West in decline. I smiled, nodded and then intercepted the turquoise eye shadow before it could be swabbed on my other eyelid.

"Hmmmm," I said. "Perhaps we could go for a more subtle palette of beiges and browns. What do you think?" The makeup artist readily agreed and quickly began removing the heavy black eyeliner and turquoise powder.

I glanced at Lara, who was fingering the ringlets that had been added to her upswept hairdo. We exchanged a look. I was sure she was thinking along the same lines I was. We wanted to be respectful. We wanted to be liked. Above all, we wanted to look our very best in keeping with our imagined "roles" as guests at the party. With some additional adjustments, I managed to look more like an elegant "Babe Paley" than a babe.

Lara and I returned to our adjoining dressing rooms to put on our gowns. There were bowls of fresh fruit on our coffee tables, and we were offered coffee and breakfast. The "boys" were down the hall, already in costume and makeup. David looked incredibly handsome in his "mutton chops" and evening jacket. Jonathan, with his hair nicely trimmed, looked very distinguished in his smart velvet tux—and made it clear he was ready to go on set and "get the job done." Jonathan, always thoroughly professional, was there to work. We all suspected we were probably an hour or more from the first setup.

But then an adjacent dressing room door popped open and a wraith-like figure with a white face and black raccoon eyes grinned at us. "Hey, hi! Alice Cooper.

How'ya doin'?" Even Jonathan was non-plussed by the sight of the famously the-atrical rock singer standing on the threshold of his dressing room.

But, who else would Barnabas Collins hire to entertain his guests other than the macabre heavy metal shock rocker, Alice Cooper? What a perfect choice! We'd heard that Johnny Depp had made a surprise impromptu appearance playing with Alice Cooper's band the previous weekend, but had no idea he'd be filming with us. Then Cheryl, Coop's wife of 35 years, joined us in the hallway and we stood in a tight group talking until we were called to the set. They were great fun and also big fans of the original series, so we all snapped photos of each other.

When we arrived on the sound stage, Tim Burton once again immediately stepped forward to greet us. The drawing room set we'd visited two days earlier was now lit, and a mirrored disco ball twirled over the ballroom. Round tables with checkered cloths were set around a dance floor, and at the top of the stairs Alice Cooper's band equipment was set up for their performance. Katterli Frauenfelder, a co-producer and the 1st A.D., ushered us up a short flight of stairs to the main entrance of Collinwood. Johnny Depp stood just inside the doorway, his hands poised on the wolf's-head cane, watching us approach. Courtly, and completely in character, Depp greeted us—and that, essentially, was to be our first scene.

We rehearsed and were about to go for a take, when Burton decided to make an adjustment that would take a few minutes. Katterli offered Jonathan a chair, which he abruptly refused. "A chair? I don't need a chair. I'm here to work! Let's just do this!"

Lara and I exchanged a quick look, then glanced at Johnny Depp. With the subtlest of gestures, he caught Tim Burton's eye and murmured softly. A moment later we were back in position, going for a take. I smiled and gave Jonathan's arm an encouraging squeeze.

Three takes later, Jonathan assured Tim Burton that he "had quite enough now," and that was it. "Oh, dear," I mumbled, and felt like adding Peggy Lee's refrain, "*is that all there is?*"

But, no, fortunately, it was not. After the first scene, Jonathan retired to his dressing room to rest. Lara and I were sent off to a quiet corner of the studio to tape press interviews. Eventually we found ourselves shepherded back to our dressing rooms to wait—for what, we wanted to know? How long? Within minutes the two of us were impatient to be back on the set. We wanted to be in the thick of it, watching Alice Cooper perform. I wanted to meet pretty, blond Bella Heathcote, the

Australian actress playing the young governess. Lara longed to chat with Eva Green, the French actress playing Angelique. This was our only chance.

Behaving like wayward school-girls, we commandeered the driver of an electric cart to haul us back to the soundstage. We sneaked in through the padded doors, mingled with the dress extras and tried to look like we belonged. When we were caught, we literally begged not to be sent back to

DRESSING ROOM: JONATHAN FRID, ALICE COOPER, KATHRYN LEIGH SCOTT AND DAVID SELBY.

KATHRYN LEIGH SCOTT, MICHELLE PFEIFFER
AND LARA PARKER.

our rooms. Eventually, kind Katerli gave permission for us to remain and had chairs set up for us next to Alice Cooper. While he was on stage performing in a strait jacket, we watched the action on a monitor with his pretty, down-to-earth wife, Cheryl.

Until we were rounded up later in the day to film another scene, Lara, David and I hovered in the "backstage" area chatting with the other actors. Helena Bonham Carter, playing Dr. Hoffman, wanted to hear all about Grayson Hall. Lara and I were delighted to accommodate her. For nearly an hour, we laughed and shared stories. Helena told us she hadn't been sure if Tim wanted her in the film, but then asked her to read the script. She did, and found the ideal role she was sure Tim had in mind for her to play. It wasn't until she was in Hollywood walking the red carpet at the Academy Awards that Richard Zanuck told her, "No, not Angelique! Dr. Hoffman!" I was thrilled when she mentioned she'd seen copies of my *Dark Shadows* books on Tim Burton's desk.

By that time, Lara and I had given it up and become wide-eyed "fans" of the new *Dark Shadows* cast. Michelle Pfeiffer—taller, slimmer and more beautiful than one could imagine—endeared herself by confiding that she had watched many of the 1,225 episodes of the series on a DVD player in the makeup room.

Lara had a chance to talk with Eva Green, and I met lovely Bella, only a year older than I was when I played Josette DuPrés. Though younger than the original character, fourteen-year-old Chloe Moretz reminded Lara and I of Nancy Barrett, who played impetuous Caroline Stoddard in our series. Gulliver "Gully" McGrath, the grownup young actor playing David Collins, captivated all of us.

When we completed our last scene, Tim Burton clapped his hands and said, "Everyone, the original cast of *Dark Shadows*!" After a round of applause, handshakes and a few hugs, we headed back to our dressing rooms. I still felt like crooning the Lieber and Stoller lyrics, "Is that's all there is…my friend?" I wanted more

As Lara and I walked across the studio lot in the fading light, I put my arm around her shoulders and said, "So, for the premiere . . . Armani or Ralph Lauren?"

She smiled and said, "Oh you know me. I'll probably just make something to wear. Should we go together?"

I laughed. "Of course. Angelique and Josette, together again! We can cause all kinds of trouble."

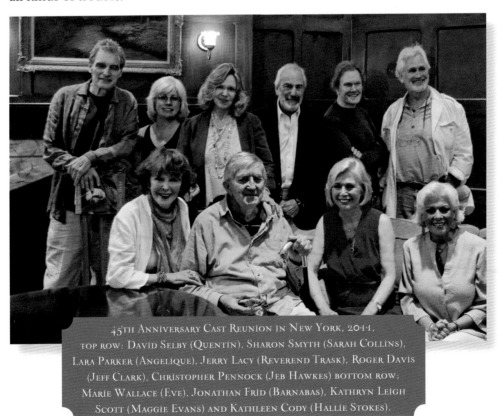

45TH ANNIVERSARY CAST REUNION IN NEW YORK, 2014, TOP ROW: DAVID SELBY (QUENTIN), SHARON SMYTH (SARAH COLLINS), LARA PARKER (ANGELIQUE), JERRY LACY (REVEREND TRASK), ROGER DAVIS (JEFF CLARK), CHRISTOPHER PENNOCK (JEB HAWKES) BOTTOM ROW: MARIE WALLACE (EVE), JONATHAN FRID (BARNABAS), KATHRYN LEIGH SCOTT (MAGGIE EVANS) AND KATHLEEN CODY (HALLIE STOKES).

Backstage
Memories of
Dark Shadows

1968, CLOCKWISE FROM TOP LEFT:
JONATHAN FRID (BARNABAS COLLINS), HUMBERT ALLEN ASTREDO
(NICHOLAS BLAIR), LARA PARKER (ANGELIQUE), LOUIS EDMONDS
(ROGER COLLINS), GRAYSON HALL (DR. JULIA HOFFMAN), JOHN KARLEN
(WILLIE LOOMIS), NANCY BARRETT (CAROLYN STODDARD), ROBERT RODAN
(ADAM), KATHRYN LEIGH SCOTT (MAGGIE EVANS) AND
THAYER DAVID (PROFESSOR T.E. STOKES).

By

KATHRYN LEIGH SCOTT

O N A RAINY FEBRUARY AFTERNOON IN 1985, I SAT LOOKING THROUGH OLD FAMILY PICTURES WITH MY PARENTS. THEY'D COME TO CALIFORNIA FROM THE SNOW AND COLD OF MINNEAPOLIS LOOKING FOR THE sun- shine I should never have promised them. But, with cake and coffee in front of a blazing log fire and the cozy sound of rain drumming against the windows, they were happy to wile away the hours paging through my scrapbooks.

Inevitably, we came across a few snapshots of old friends from *Dark Shadows* days. There was a picture of Lara Parker (Angelique) and her husband Jim Hawkins. Another of Jonathan Frid, John Karlen and me leaving the studio after work. There were snapshots sent to me by fans of various other actors, including me, standing in front of the studio signing autographs.

Sadly, I mentioned that another close friend, Joel Crothers, who had played my boy friend, Joe Haskell, had recently died. Coincidentally, only a few months before his death, Joel had bought a house near ours in the Hollywood Hills. Grayson Hall had passed away, too, only months earlier.

As I shuffled through the handful of old snapshots, it struck me that it had been almost exactly twenty years since I'd first met Dan Curtis and auditioned for *Dark Shadows*. Several readings and camera tests later, I'd been signed for the role of Maggie Evans in the ABC afternoon Gothic romance serial, which aired its first show on June 27, 1966.

That day, I spoke my very first words "You're a jerk, J..E..R..K..!" to Victoria Winters, the newly arrived governess at Collinwood, played by Alexandra Moltke. I can still remember Lela Swift, our director, telling me, "When the red light goes on, start talking!" And I can still feel the panic rising in my throat as the stage manager started his countdown, "...5...4...3...2..."

Conrad Bain was in that first show, playing the Collinsport innkeeper, and I could see him out of the corner of my eye preparing for his entrance. Also there were Joan Bennett, Louis Edmonds, Mitchell Ryan, Alexandra Moltke and Elizabeth Wilson. Most of all, I remember promising God that if He'd just help me get through that show, I'd give it all up and go back to Robbinsdale, Minnesota.

Well, He did ... and I didn't. I went on to appear in 635 of the 1,225 episodes of *Dark Shadows*.

In that mound of photographs, I found pictures of me as Maggie Evans, a waitress in a diner and later the governess at Collinwood; Josette DuPrés, intended bride of Barnabas in 1795; Lady Kitty Hampshire, an English aristocrat; Rachel Drummond, another governess, in 1897 Additionally, if you wonder how it all ended, there were pictures of me as Maggie Evans being carted off to an insane asylum in my final show of the series, episode #1109 that aired September 17, 1970. I'd "died" so many times in these various incarnations, only to return in another time period as another character. Yet, when I told Dan Curtis that I wanted to leave the show so I could move to Paris and marry my fiancé, Ben Martin, there was no "grand finale" death scene. Instead, Dan institutionalized poor Maggie hoping that I would come to my senses and not leave the show permanently.

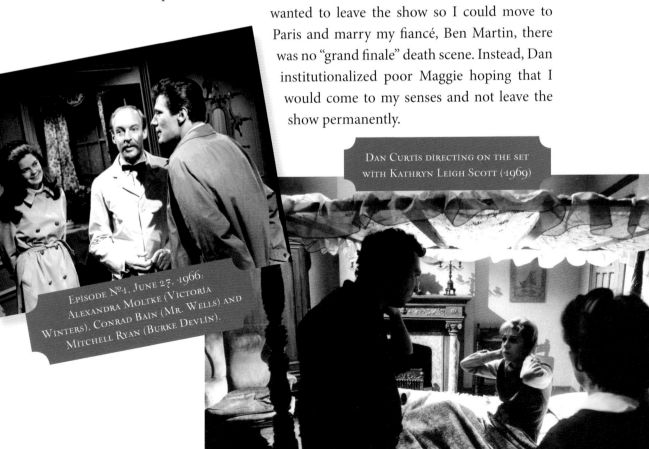

EPISODE N° 4, JUNE 27, 1966:
ALEXANDRA MOLTKE (VICTORIA WINTERS), CONRAD BAIN (MR. WELLS) AND MITCHELL RYAN (BURKE DEVLIN).

DAN CURTIS DIRECTING ON THE SET WITH KATHRYN LEIGH SCOTT (1969)

·1795·
Countess Natalie DuPres
(Grayson Hall) and Josette (Kathryn).

Dark Shadows was a huge success. During that five-year run (June 1966—April 1971) on afternoon television, the serial spawned two motion pictures, several novels, a syndicated comic strip, bubble gum cards, phonograph records and a network of fan clubs so devoted that thousands show up to attend annual cast-reunion festivals. I've been recognized as Maggie Evans on safari in Kenya, in a pub in Dublin, at a flea market in Paris, and jogging along the beach in Malibu. Even when I was playing Nurse Kelly opposite James Stewart in the London production of *Harvey*, fans came backstage to talk to me about *Dark Shadows*. No matter how many plays, films and television shows I've appeared in over the years, I will always be associated with the roles I played on *Dark Shadows*.

In the mid 1980s, I ran into Lara Parker at an audition and we decided to have lunch at a little restaurant near the studio. It was an old Hollywood haunt with signed photographs of legendary movie stars lining the walls. Your eyes automatically scanned the booths for famous faces. On our way to the table, we passed several well-known actors, all *bona-fide* celebrities compared to us. Yet when the waitress handed us menus, she did an ever-so-subtle double take and we saw that unmistakable look cross her face. By the time we got our white wine and salads, our waitress confessed that she just couldn't believe that Josette and Angelique were dining at her table.

All soap opera actors tell similar stories. Audiences develop such an intimate relationship with the characters they watch every day that they find the real-life actors portraying them very approachable. Our waitress recognized Lara and me as Angelique and Josette despite the fact she'd last seen us together on television some two decades earlier wearing 1790s wigs and costumes.

My dentist and I never talked about my early life as a vampire's object of affection, but one afternoon in the waiting room I overheard him tell a patient, "If you stick around a minute you'll see Maggie Evans walk in." Several young casting directors have confessed to bringing me in for an interview because "you're not going to believe this, but I used to rush home from grade school to watch you!"

At 6:15 one morning I was racing to catch a flight to Minneapolis when a young security agent glanced at me and said, "Gosh, Maggie Evans!" Then he said, "Good morning, Miss Scott."

"How in the world did you recognize me?" I asked. "I was in a mini-skirt, false eyelashes, long hair . . . I can't believe it!"

He looked genuinely puzzled. "Oh, I don't think any of you have changed a bit," he said, and added that David Selby had walked through his security check only weeks before.

The doomed vampire vision of Josette DuPres, played by Kathryn Leigh Scott in the 1795 storyline. (1968)

I never can believe how reverently and affectionately the show is remembered. "Do you ever see Barnabas?" I'm asked. "What was Widows' Hill like?" "I named my kitten Josette."

Back in the autumn of 1970 when I left the show, I would never have guessed *Dark Shadows* would enjoy such lasting popularity. I only knew that I was terribly in love and wanted desperately to marry and move to Paris. Dan Curtis tried to discourage me from going to Europe and warned me that I'd probably never find work as an actress there. Besides, in addition to playing in the serial, I also had a major role in the MGM film *House of Dark Shadows* that was just being released. Dan thought I was mad to leave New York and abandon a career that was just getting started.

But I was determined and by the autumn of 1970 I was living in an apartment in Paris near Napoleon's tomb, a popular tourist attraction. On my way home one morning from French classes, I'd shopped at a street market and filled my straw basket with fruit, cheese and bread. As I approached my front door, a middle-aged man stepped out of an American Express tour bus and focused his movie camera on me. Behind him, a woman called out, "Get her quick, honey! She's so typical-looking!" It pleased me. I was very happy in my new role as a Parisian housewife.

That winter, *La Fiancée du Vampire* (the French dubbed version of *House of Dark Shadows*) was playing on the *Champs Elysées* and I watched myself dubbed in French. But I was already speaking French as an actress playing twins in a French film, *L'Alfomega*. As soon

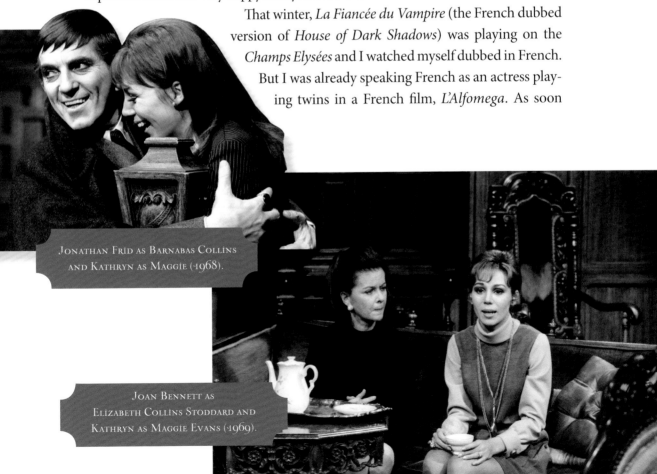

JONATHAN FRID AS BARNABAS COLLINS
AND KATHRYN AS MAGGIE (1968).

JOAN BENNETT AS
ELIZABETH COLLINS STODDARD AND
KATHRYN AS MAGGIE EVANS (1969).

HOUSE OF DARK SHADOWS: JONATHAN FRID AS BARNABAS AND KATHRYN AS MAGGIE.

THEATRE IN PARIS SCREENING HOUSE OF DARK SHADOWS IN FRENCH.

as I was hired for my first acting job in Paris, I wrote to Dan Curtis telling him I hadn't made such a dreadful mistake after all. But as pleased as I was to be working in France, I was also homesick for New York and missed my friends on the show.

Months later I was shocked to hear that *Dark Shadows* was going off the air. I wept with disappointment, realizing I'd harbored the notion that one day I would return to New York and resume my role. Maggie could come home from her insane asylum and all would be as it was. In fact, I continued to work as an actress in France and England for another seven years before returning to the U.S. to work on a feature film and then a television series. In the meantime, I stayed in touch with my *Dark Shadows* colleagues.

Dark Shadows was my first professional acting job. After graduating from the American Academy of Dramatic Arts. I signed with a theatrical agent, Richard Bauman, who'd seen me work in a student production. I bought myself a pink linen suit, very high-heeled shoes and twisted my hair into an elaborate French chignon. In those days, we all tried to look like Jackie Kennedy. I set out pounding the pavements, carrying my brand new 8 x 10 glossies and a rather skimpy resume, eager to audition for anything that came my way.

I also signed with another agent, who specialized in TV commercials. She was elderly, slightly deaf, had neon-yellow hair, and worked by herself out of a single shabby room in a scruffy building on Eighth Avenue. She had a couple of bright yellow filing cabinets, a telephone, and a rickety desk with a box of Lady Scott tissues on it. On my first visit to her office, she called a casting director too submit me for a hairspray commercial. She forgot my name during the course of the introduction, but kept telling them how wonderful I was while I mouthed my name again and again. Finally I spelled it: "K..R..I..N..G..S..T..A..D..! KATHRYN KRINGSTAD!"

She stared at me, cupped her hand over the phone and asked, "What kinda name is that?" She looked down at the box of tissues and told the casting director my name was "Kathryn Scott." I went to the audition, told them my name was "Kringstad," but that I was listed as "Scott." The bored receptionist asked, "So, who are ya then?"

I got the job. At Screen Actors Guild I explained the saga of my name change to the woman who was signing me up and she said, "So, you wanna know should ya be Scott or—what's that other one?"

I should never have changed my name and regret doing so. My parents couldn't understand it either, but in the end I said, "Look, if I do anything awful with my life, at least you won't be embarrassed to read my name in the papers." Meanwhile the elderly agent with the phosphorescent hair died within weeks of renaming me after a box of facial tissues, and I don't even remember *her* name.

On the brighter side, depending upon her shopping tastes, I could've been called Kathryn Kleenex.

Richard Bauman managed to set up quite a few interviews for me, mostly "go-sees"– general meetings with casting directors, which in those days meant performing short prepared scenes in someone's office. One such "go-see" led to an interview with Dan Curtis. At that first audition for *Dark Shadows* I met Louis Edmonds and Alexandra Moltke in the reception room. There were several other readings and later two camera tests before I was offered the role of Maggie Evans. During that time I worked in summer stock in Roanoke, Virginia; made my first TV commercial; filmed a screen test in Hollywood and began rehearsals for a play to be presented in the first season of the Eugene O'Neil Festival in Waterbury, Connecticut.

Everything seemed to happen at once. I auditioned for Eleanor Kilgallen in New York City and it seemed the next minute I was flying to Hollywood with two

KATHRYN LEIGH SCOTT
1960s PUBLICITY PHOTOS

other young actresses to test for a Universal Studios contract. The whole trip was carefully programmed from the moment we left New York. Studio drivers chauffeured us from the airport to the hotel, to restaurants, to rehearsals, to hair, makeup and wardrobe appointments, and finally to the big moment in front of the camera.

Then, as magically as it had begun, it was over. No more dressing-room trailers or chauffeur-driven limos. All I had was the horrendous memory of catching a last-minute glimpse of myself in a mirror before I was shoved in front of the camera. I looked godawful in pancake makeup and a hairdo not seen since the 1940s. My skinny five-foot-seven body had been stuffed into a matronly brocade suit retrieved from the wardrobe warehouse. I looked absurd!

I stood in the melting sun surrounded by cavernous gray-cement sound stages with wardrobe slung over my arm and nowhere to go. With a sinking feeling in my stomach and an overwhelming desire to flee back to New York City, I finally found a phone and called my agent. "Come on home," he said. "You've got another camera test for Dan Curtis Monday morning. You'll find a script for *Dark Shadows* on your doorstep."

I still have that script with the audition scenes and a memo from Richard Bauman with instructions for my camera tests on May 2 and 3, 1966. In his memo, Richard casually suggested that I "drop by Bloomingdale's cosmetics department for a demonstration makeover. I believe there's some sort of powder the models use to hollow out their cheeks. You might give it a try."

I knew, short of extracting every molar in my mouth, there wasn't a hope I'd ever have glamorous sunken cheeks. Blusher was not going to do the trick. I also had a couple of prominent front teeth, which, along with my "baby pudge" face, made me look like a cheerful chipmunk. I wished with all my heart that my mother had insisted upon braces when I was a kid. Richard Bauman went on to suggest that I lower my voice, watch my inflections and not move my face around too much. I followed his instructions to the letter and the test went well. But still no casting decisions were made.

I began rehearsals for *The Contrast*, an early American Restoration style play to be directed by Worthington Miner at the Eugene O'Neil Festival. Two weeks into rehearsal, Worthington Miner (whose son, Peter Miner, would later become one of the *Dark Shadows* producers) told me I would be testing again for the show. Early one morning I taped a scene with Mitch Ryan and another actor, both of whom were auditioning for the role of Burke Devlin. Afterwards, Mitch, the other actor and I all went to Joe Allen, the well-known actor's hangout, for a late breakfast. When I arrived at rehearsals for *The Contrast*, Worthington Miner took me aside and told me to call my agent, that I'd got the role of Maggie.

"I'll still be able to do *The Contrast*, won't I?" I hadn't a clue what the work that I'd been auditioning for all those months would be like. My sole experience on camera had been screen tests and a day's work filming a TV commercial. Mr. Miner told me they'd try to work it out. I later discovered that father and son had discussed the matter the night before my final test for *Dark Shadows*, when it already looked as though I'd be selected. In effect, they had decided my future. The negotiations were handled very quickly and I happily signed my contract.

I called my parents in Robbinsdale from a noisy phone booth on Broadway near Times Square to tell them the good news. I was bubbling with excitement while my mother kept asking, "Are you sure they really want you? Have you signed anything?" In the end, finally believing my good luck, my mother said, "Just don't get carried away now and give up your part-time job." (My "bread and butter" job at the time was working as a Bunny at the Playboy Club!)

My agent treated me to lunch that day at Howard Johnson's on 46th Street and Broadway. Richard advised me about saving money, getting my teeth straightened and not letting my head get turned from simply concentrating on my work.

"This is only the beginning", he said. I'm grateful to this day for his sober guidance. I appreciated my mother's advice as well and waited several weeks before I quit my Bunny job.

I came in with my lines learned for the read through of the first episode of *Dark Shadows*. Rehearsals were held in the Terrace Room of the Empire Hotel, a stale old Broadway Rose, down on her heels and well past her prime. It was dark and seedy and smelled bad and I got lost in the maze of corridors trying to find the ballroom where rehearsals were to be held. The best piece of news was free coffee and Danish pastry to calm my nerves. Since then, it's always cheered me to find coffee and Danish available at rehearsals.

Introductions were made and everyone seemed just as skittish and apprehensive as I was. There was lots of nervous laughter and bright chatter. I felt immediate relief when I saw the familiar taped diagram of the set on the floor, which reminded me of every other rehearsal stage I'd ever seen. I realized then that I'd been expecting the cameras and lights that had greeted me in Hollywood when I arrived for rehearsals on the sound stage.

I saw Joan Bennett sitting alone at a table in the corner, dressed in a pink suit. She wore bright-blue-tinted glasses and some of the most beautiful jewelry I'd ever seen. I believe it was Nancy Barrett (Carolyn Stoddard) who introduced us. Joan greeted me warmly. Her voice was rich and cultured, her diction perfect, the product of early sound-stage motion picture training. She eyed the Danish in my hand (my second or third that morning), and suggested that the figure one had before twenty-one is the

1966:
JOAN BENNETT AS ELIZABETH COLLINS STODDARD; LOUIS EDMONDS AS ROGER COLLINS; NANCY BARRETT AS CAROLYN STODDARD; AND ALEXANDRA MOLTKE AS VICTORIA WINTERS.

1966:
DAVID HENESY AS DAVID COLLINS,
ALEXANDRA MOLTKE AS VICTORIA WINTERS
AND LOUIS EDMONDS AS ROGER COLLINS.

figure one should keep a lifetime. The cheese Danish slid off my hand and found its way into a wastebasket. Joan, then in her late fifties, was as trim and elegant as a woman less than half her age. She'd often arrive at the studio carrying a container of homemade chicken soup in a small Tiffany shopping bag.

The first rehearsal was a bit traumatizing as I'd never worked on original material before. Scripts came from Samuel French and dialogue was seldom altered. But after the first read-through, entire lines of dialogue were struck out, sometimes whole pages, to fit the rigidly-timed half-hour format. Worse, the character of Maggie Evans became a stranger to me. How could I have made it through all of those auditions and camera tests and still feel so unconnected to the role?

Lela Swift was our first director, and she remained with us throughout the entire run of the series. What a gift! She was wonderful working with actors. Her considerable technical skill had been honed through years of directing early live television. Lela spent a great deal of time working with me to shape Maggie Evans into the edgy, fast-talking waitress at the Collinsport diner. Lela saw Maggie as "a crackling young Eve Arden."

"Sling those words out like hash!" Lela told me. "Where's that chip on your shoulder?"

I was so willing, but also overwhelmed by the newness of everything. Lela kept reminding me that Maggie's father "is an alcoholic, an itinerant painter, a melancholy dreamer. Maggie is the breadwinner, the stable force in the household, a position she resents because it holds her back from pursuing her own dreams." There was so much richness to the character, but I felt like a child Lela had to guide step by step.

We rehearsed the first five shows for about a week at the Empire Hotel before we went into the studio. This pre-production period was also used to assemble wardrobe and do camera tests for makeup. I'd often have lunch with Nancy Barrett and Joel Crothers, both of whom had more camera experience than I did. I listened closely to them, picking up bits and pieces of information from the casual small talk. Their relaxed, positive, straightforward approach to the work made an impression on me. They didn't take themselves too seriously and knew how to pace themselves. Joel took me aside one day and told me to take it easy. "You've got all day to get it together so don't rush for results."

Our first show was recorded June 13, 1966. In the very early days, we taped in black and white at ABC-TV Studio Two at 24 West 67th Street, a short walk from the 63rd Street rehearsal room at the Empire hotel. The vast studio on 67th Street, painted submarine gray, was so disorienting that I frequently got lost in the winding corridors. I was relieved when we moved to our own studio on 53rd Street some months later.

At the first taping, a lump the size of a boulder lodged itself in my throat. I was so nervous I wondered if I'd manage to squeeze out any words. At the last minute I'd been fitted with a short blond wig because Dan Curtis thought that with my own dark hair I too closely resembled Alexandra Moltke (Victoria Winters). Lela pushed up the sleeves on the sweater I wore over my uniform and reminded me that I was a waitress and my job was to clean the counter, not act. Producer Bob Costello walked by, making final checks before going into the control booth. He glanced my way and I was sure he was thinking that I wasn't going to make it.

That moment before an actor walks out on stage, or waits for the red light on the camera to blink on, is a potent mixture of pumped-up exhilaration and mind-numbing terror. You can feel like brittle, dry spaghetti straight out of the box and the limp, cooked stuff all at the same time. I was sure I was going to die (if only I could!). Yet as soon as I started to push a damp cloth across the counter, I gathered the calm and concentration needed to stay focused.

Maggie's wig was soon discarded. One day Dan saw me arrive for rehearsal and decided he liked my own hair better than the blond wig. Over Lela Swift's very vocal objections, Maggie appeared, without explanation, in long dark hair instead of short blond hair. It was a small thing, but a significant indication of what was to come. Dan never let anything stop him from making changes, trying something new.

The whole format of *Dark Shadows* was innovative; there was no precedent for our style of afternoon television show. Dan told me the genesis of *Dark Shadows* was a dream he'd had when he was a guest at an old country house, which was supposedly haunted by the ghost of a woman. Later he developed the story of a young girl on a train, huddled against the window and looking out into the brooding night as she passed through the small New England villages. She was a quiet, dreamy girl, with long, flowing hair. As she watched her reflection in the window of the speeding train, she thought:

My name is Victoria Winters. I am going on a journey that will bring me to a strange, dark house on the edge of the sea at Widows' Hill. There, I am going to be a governess to a young boy and the companion of a mysterious woman.

1966:
NANCY BARRETT AS CAROLYN STODDARD
AND MITCHELL RYAN AS BURKE DEVLIN.

Alexandra Moltke, playing Victoria Winters, read the opening narration of the episodes for the first year or so. One day, again without explanation, another actor was assigned to record the introduction. The reason was simple enough and purely economical: If Alex didn't appear in the episode but spoke the opening narration, she still had to be paid for the show. From that time on, we all took turns doing the introduction, the only rule being that the narrator couldn't appear in the opening scene.

Victoria Winters, so the story went, had been abandoned at a foundling home in the dead of winter at the age of two months with a note attached to her blanket that read: "Her name is Victoria. I can no longer take care of her." By the age of twenty, Victoria had earned her teaching certificate and was now working at the orphanage where she'd been raised. Because of a vague premonition that it might lead her to learn more about her background, she accepted the position of governess to a little boy, the nephew of wealthy and reclusive Elizabeth Collins Stoddard.

She took the overnight train to Collinsport and so began Victoria Winters' journey on June 27, 1966 as written by Art Wallace and directed by Lela Swift

THE FIERY PORTRAIT OF
LAURA COLLINS (DIANA MILLAY) AND
SON DAVID COLLINS (DAVID HENESY).

. . . a journey to link my past with my future . . . a journey that is bringing me closer to a world I've never known . . . to darkness and strangeness that I hope will open the doors of life to me. A journey to people I've never met . . . people who, tonight, are still only shadows in my mind, but who will soon fill the days and nights of my tomorrows . . .

All the elements we've come to associate with *Dark Shadows* were there from the beginning: Bob Cobert's eerie, brooding music; the atmosphere of mystery and melancholy created by Sy Tomashoff's massive carved oak, Gothic interiors for Collinwood; Mel Handelsman's evocative lighting; the plaintive yearning of the voice-over introduction; and, of course, many of the actors who would remain with the show throughout most or all of its run—Joan Bennett, Louis Edmonds, Nancy Barrett, David Henesy and me. Alexandra Moltke stayed with the show only about two and a half years. Mitch Ryan, Clarice Blackburn, Thayer David and Joel Crothers were also important early cast members, who contributed to the style and tone of *Dark Shadows*.

During the first several months, the story had entirely to do with the intrigues of the grand old Collins family of Collinsport, Maine. Several of us worked up "Down East" accents which were immediately denounced by Dan: "You guys sound like a bunch'a foreigners!" One of the story lines I specifically remember had to do with some mysterious "tampering of the bleeder valve on Roger Collins' master brake cylinder." All of us spoke this line, but few of us had any idea what it meant.

Burke Devlin, the sexy bad guy, was played by Mitch Ryan. One of the plot lines had him nearly seducing Victoria Winters and thereby earning the jealous wrath of Carolyn Stoddard, played by Nancy Barrett. This story introduced a pen, a gift from Burke to Carolyn, that made the rounds for weeks causing suspicion, misunderstandings, possibly even murder. It was stolen, recovered, buried, found and even tossed into the ravine at the bottom of Widows' Hill, where someone

1966:
ROGER COLLINS (LOUIS EDMONDS) AND
VICTORIA WINTERS (ALEXANDRA MOLTKE);
BURKE DEVLIN (MITCHELL RYAN) AND
WILBUR STRAKE (JOSEPH JULIAN).

managed to retrieve it before it abruptly vanished from the storyline.

Frank Schofield played sea captain Bill Malloy, who seemed to occupy our lives for months on end, even long after his death. Dripping with seaweed, he returned from the grave and became our first resident ghost. By January of 1967, we were dealing with the story of the Phoenix consumed in flames and reborn out of the ashes to become Laura Collins (played by Diana Millay), mother of David Collins. Josette DuPrés had also made her ghostly appearance.

1968:
KATHRYN LEIGH SCOTT AS MAGGIE EVANS
AND TV SWEETHEART JOEL CROTHERS
AS JOE HASKELL.

Arch and aristocratic Roger Collins was played to delicious perfection by arch and aristocratic Louis Edmonds. Brother/sister scenes between Louis and Joan were a study in icy disdain; no one could sneer like Louis, especially when he was wearing a smoking jacket and swirling a snifter of brandy.

In the final shot of one episode, Roger Collins was supposed to lean against the drawing room mantel, brandy glass in hand. My scenes for the day were completed and I had gone upstairs to my dressing room, breaking the cardinal rule we all disobeyed: taking off our costumes before the final clearance had been given. As I walked down the hall I saw Louis Edmonds standing in his dressing room stripped down to his T-shirt, shorts and socks—but he still had another scene to play! At that moment, June, the wardrobe mistress, rushed up the stairs in a panic, shouting, "Where's Louis?" Louis then realized that he hadn't yet finished the day's episode and ran for the stairs. Everyone hurried after him, no one wanting to miss the unforgettable moment of seeing Louis in extreme close-up leaning against the mantel sipping brandy wearing only socks, undershorts, a smoking jacket and a look of smug disdain.

Most of my scenes took place at work in the diner, at home with my often-drunk Pop (portrayed by David Ford), or at the Blue Whale tavern on dates with my boyfriend, Joe Haskell, played by Joel Crothers. Joel was my best friend on and off camera. I dated Ben Martin, a *Time* magazine photographer, whenever he was in town, which was almost never, because he was usually off on assignment to some far-flung trouble spot in the world. The rest of the time, Joel and I palled around. One day I told Joel that Ben had finished working on a *Time* assignment in West Africa and was heading for Rome. Since I had some time off, I decided to fly over to see Ben and had made last-minute reservations on an Alitalia flight leaving that night. About seven o'clock that evening, Joel arrived at my door with a suitcase and tickets in hand to join me for the flight to Rome.

We caused quite a sensation aboard that plane—Maggie and Joe running off together! It was the first time I think I realized how popular the show was becoming. The following morning, a very surprised Ben picked us up at Fiumincino Airport. The three of us squeezed into Ben's MGB-GT for the drive into the city. We found a hotel room for Joel and then Ben and I went shopping in a leather goods store. I'd arrived with my clothing in a shopping bag because I wanted to buy some fine Italian luggage.

While Ben worked, Joel and I went sightseeing. At the Vatican we were prevented from entering because of my miniskirt. At Joel's suggestion, I unzipped the skirt and let it hang on my hips with three inches of bare belly showing. Then, suitably attired, we toured the Museum and Basilica.

Dark Shadows moved to ABC TV Studio 16 at 433 West 53rd Street, a two-story brick building wedged between tenements on a street of small shops and cafes in a neighborhood then known as Hell's Kitchen. There was an elementary school across the street and a Pentacostal Church nearby. One of my favorite memories is of rising just after dawn and making my way across town through the quiet, almost deserted streets to the studio.

Rehearsals started promptly at eight o'clock. We all arrived several minutes early to tank up on coffee and Danish. Most of us had our lines learned for blocking rehearsals and didn't bother to carry scripts. A few preferred to write down their moves and learn dialogue during the 10:30 breakfast break. The morning session usually allowed us time to block the show completely and have one or two run-throughs. Folding metal chairs represented tables and beds—later, coffins and secret panels. The fluorescent lighting made us all look a little green.

Even in the early days, the stories we did were the stuff of Gothic romance and mystery, with heightened reality and an other-worldly, old-fashioned quality to the drama. We didn't knock knees at coffee tables in suburban living rooms

1966: *Dark Shadows* studio taping; Joan Bennett & Alexandra Moltke.

gossiping about romantic intrigues as happened on the other daytime soaps. As I've mentioned, there were indications early on that we were heading into the world of horror and fantasy. I remember the day when we finally embraced the supernatural—or, some would say, stumbled into it.

The ghost of Bill Malloy appeared to Victoria . . . and that was the turning point, as far as Lela Swift was concerned. Lela stopped the read-through rehearsal and said, "We've crossed over. I wonder if Dan knows we're doing a ghost story here?" But there was no turning back. Soon we welcomed the ghost of Josette and the mysterious Phoenix creature, Laura Collins.

At 10:30 we'd all go our separate ways. Those of us who had elaborate special effects makeup or period coiffures went directly to makeup and hair dressing, while others retired to their dressing rooms to learn lines or take a short nap. Thayer David generally went out to breakfast at a greasy spoon on the corner that served the usual coffeehouse menu. Mitch Ryan and I joined Thayer one day and watched him tuck away eggs, bacon, pancakes, sausage, a bowl of soup, apple pie *a la mode* and order a chocolate malt, a six-pack of 7UP and some chocolate cake "to go." His appetite was truly inspiring.

JOAN BENNETT AS ELIZABETH AND
ALEXANDRA MOLTKE AS VICTORIA

1967
THE PORTRAIT OF JOSETTE DUPRES

By 11:30 everyone was downstairs in the studio blocking scenes for camera. I was usually wearing a robe with my hair in curlers and my makeup half done for camera blocking. I can hear it now—the buzz of conversation, the slap of camera cables snaking across the floor and the voice over the loudspeaker: "Stop, take it back to your cross and for God's sake rise slower out of that chair!" Later, when we got into "ghosts and ghoulies," the directions were truly chilling. "When the hand pokes out of the grave, turn into camera three and scream." But, of course.

It became second nature to make note of marks to hit and all the other technical details one had to keep in mind. Camera marks were critical, particularly when we were using special effects involving chromakey, a process that allows an object in another place to be superimposed in a scene. The superimposed object is placed against a plain blue or green background and, by electronic means, manipulated to an exact spot where it appears to be part of the primary scene. In one particularly complex sequence, Jonathan and I played a scene together in which we could not see each other. Against a chromakey screen, I stood "floating" above Barnabas, who was in Josette's room at the other end of the studio. On screen, it appeared we were in the same room together as Josette "disappeared" into her portrait.

BARNABAS AND MAGGIE

Chromakey became commonplace. We used it when the vampire appeared as a bat and for the flames consuming Angelique. Occasionally we used the whole bag of tricks: lightening, thunder, giant fans, smoke pots, pails of dry ice and—my favorite—a machine that made airy cobwebs out of a sticky glue substance that smelled like cheap bubble gum. All of these special effects seem primitive now, but in the mid-1960s they were cutting edge.

Early on it was decided that vampires would crawl out of their coffins off camera. There was simply no way to sling one leg, then the other and hoist oneself to the floor without looking ridiculous—especially wearing a cape. Jonathan was none too happy that his coffin was just a touch too short to lie in comfortably. It was also impossible to speak with fangs. Whenever anybody had to insert fangs, the camera stayed on the other actor, who kept talking until the teeth were in place.

1967:
KATHRYN AS VAMPIRE VICTIM
MAGGIE EVANS.

I was heartbroken when my turn came to wear fangs and I wasn't given any. I did become a vampire ("once bitten" and all that) but I wasn't fitted with proper fangs—bridgework that I could pop in and out like Jonathan and Lara did. I think the plotline caught us all off guard and no one thought ahead to send me to the dentist. But makeup man Vincent Loscalzo to the rescue! When the appropriate moment arrived, I'd duck off camera, quickly wipe my incisors dry and Vinnie would stand ready with eyelash glue to paste two false fingernails in place over my teeth. My upper lip held the ersatz fangs in place. Lara got to keep her fangs, and even wore them for a guest appearance on Johnny Carson's *The Tonight Show*.

What I did manage to keep is a Latex patch with two fang holes that makeup artist Dick Smith applied to my neck after Barnabas bit me in *House of Dark Shadows* (1970). To create a mold for the scar, Dick Smith used a piece of the veal scaloppini his wife was preparing for their dinner. He punctured the slice of raw veal with a meat fork to create fang marks and then used it for a Latex cast. I'd never part with my precious vintage scar. It resides in a box with the Mintakan pointy ears and forehead made for me by Michael Westmore to wear in an episode of *Star Trek: The Next Generation*.

Wearing that gruesome wound on my neck and the grotesque Josette horror makeup never bothered me. During the filming of *House of Dark Shadows*, it didn't upset me when the special-effects crew fitted Jonathan with a rubber bladder under his shirt so they could pump blood through the wound after a wooden stake pierced his heart. It was sickening to see but, after watching the lengthy set-up for the scene, I was prepared for the effect. Unfortunately, I wasn't so cool-headed about climbing into a coffin.

During one of the episodes of the series, I had to lie in a casket. I hadn't given it a thought when I read the script or even considered what my reaction might be to the real coffin. Three metal folding chairs stood in for the casket during rehearsals for the scene. When we assembled in the studio for camera blocking, Bob Costello asked me to climb into the casket so they could position it for lighting. It was the real thing, de luxe tufted-white-satin lining and all, straight out of a mortuary. My

heart started to pound as soon as I saw it. I began to giggle as I stretched out and crossed my arms, ashamed of the overwhelming panic that seized me. Then they closed the lid to see if I could breathe through the air vents. I don't remember a thing after that until I found myself on the other side of the studio, trembling and trying to breathe. I fought to calm myself and tried to explain my curious behavior, assuring everyone that I was just fine. But I wasn't at all sure I'd be able to get through that scene. It was a dreadful experience and I had visions of Maggie unaccountably rising from the dead on camera to everyone's amazement. Lying

TOP: 1969 REHEARSAL:
KATHRYN LEIGH SCOTT, DON BRISCOE,
NANCY BARRETT AND JOAN BENNETT.

BOTTOM: 1969: STUDIO CONTROL ROOM.

in that casket, I mentally balanced my checkbook, planned a dinner-party menu, prayed, and somehow got through the show.

During camera blocking, cue lights were set up outside doors when an actor had to make an entrance and couldn't hear the dialogue or see the stage manager's signal. Quick costume changes were laid out and timed if an actor had to sprint from one set to another. All these arrangements were made during the blocking rehearsal and refined during the run-through and dress rehearsal. Once the taping commenced, even the commercial breaks were rolled into the half-hour program.

The run-through, commonly called the "stumble-through," started at 1:15. Still in robes and sneakers, we tried to get through without stopping the flow of action. Our chances of accomplishing this were next to nil. There was also a certain amount of horsing around: rude notes found in drawers, short-sheeted beds, silly things hanging in closets or stuffed in coffins. Normally, everything went wrong and any attempt at concentrating on performance was pointless. The notion that we'd have any sort of show to tape in two hours seemed very remote.

In truth, we let things go wrong. If anything needed fixing, now was the time to do it. Technical trouble spots and how to deal with potential malfunctions were tucked away in some recess of the mind. We got our notes from the director, often including dialogue cuts, on the run as we prepared for dress rehearsal at 2:15. The pace picked up as everyone hurried to get into costume. Throughout the day, actors had gathered in pairs and groups to run lines and talk over their scenes. Now it was time to trust the work and hope the technical elements would fall into place.

We all have different ways of working, and those differences were always most evident during dress rehearsal. For some it was the last chance to explore, to try another choice before the "real thing." Others paced themselves carefully: no real tears, no full-throttle screams until show time. Some actors were completely made up and costumed, requiring only a dusting of powder before air time, while others purposely left in curlers or kept tissues inside their collars as if to keep themselves in a rehearsal state of mind. Some actors rehearse everything minutely; their performance grows steadily, layer by layer, and nothing is left to chance. Others, wary of repetition, simply mark their moves, valuing the freshness and spontaneity of the on-air moment. Still others internalize everything, living the character throughout the day so the work unfolds naturally and seamlessly.

Dark Shadows cast members represented every sort of working method but, whatever our individual styles, we worked well together. The directors, too, each had a different approach, but it was Henry Kaplan who introduced a unique vocabulary. "Transish!" he'd holler, and that was our cue to change intent or action. Sometimes he'd scowl and raise one imperious bushy eyebrow to ask, "That's the way you're gonna do it?" Emphatically not, and we'd scramble to come up with something else.

It was obvious that Hank loved working with actors. "Alright, children, let's gather" signaled the start of rehearsal. Then, like a grand maestro, he'd wave his arms and wiggle his extravagant eyebrows to indicate the rhythmic flow of the scene. Occasionally, he'd flinch as though he'd heard a sour note and command, "Cut! Transish! And if I don't see it, you don't get the close-up!" When we finished an episode, Henry would make a circuit of the dressing rooms giving grades for the day's performance. He'd fix you with the look of a stern schoolmaster, pause dramatically and then articulate very clearly, "B-plus!" Now and again, there was an "improvement needed" or "Dare I say it, A-minus!" We loved Henry and his antic behavior.

Some people didn't want to kiss first thing in the morning. As the kiss approached, the actors would often back three feet apart, turn to the director and announce, "I believe this is where we kiss." Some actors put the kiss off until dress rehearsal. Some were so familiar with each other's lips, they postponed the event like an old married couple until air-time. One actor simply stopped the scene, sprayed Binaca breath freshener in his mouth and swung into the kissing part as though pausing to tie his shoelaces before a five-hundred-meter hurdle race.

Others really got into it from eight a.m. on and you could be pretty sure there was more going on than dedication to craft.

During the first year of *Dark Shadows* we were plagued by a mysterious noise during dress rehearsal, a loud wheezing rumble that sounded like an old sewing machine. It was terribly irritating, but fortunately the sound usually disappeared during taping. One day, Maggie visited Collinwood and I was left cooling my heels for several minutes outside the grand entrance, which was next to the TelePrompTer station. The technician was wearing earphones and couldn't hear the hideous racket, but I could and decided to investigate. I squeezed behind a flat to the tiny recess behind the drawing room fireplace at Collinwood. There was old Joe, a painter who'd come to work at dawn, leaning back in a folding metal chair, his feet propped up on the fire extinguisher and the fuel canister, his mouth open, his eyes closed, enjoying a noisy siesta. I didn't wake him. I just sneaked back in time to make my entrance. After the taping I told George DiCenzo, our associate producer, about my discovery. Arrangements were made and old Joe was assigned a new location for his afternoon nap.

Frantic isn't quite the word, but voices grew louder and the pace more hectic during that half hour before taping at 3:15. It was "organized chaos" as the camera crew met in the rehearsal room for notes while the actors rushed from dressing rooms to the hair and makeup departments for last minute preparations. When the actors finally assembled for notes, Vinnie, Irene Hamalain (later Edith Tilles) and June usually tagged along. We fidgeted and fussed, getting a button sewed on, poking curls in place, smearing on more lip gloss as we absorbed those last minute instructions.

"Pick up your cues!"

1966: CAMERAMAN STUART GOODMAN;
1968: GRAYSON HALL, MARIE WALLACE,
JONATHAN FRID AND HUMBERT ALLEN ASTREDO.

1967: John Sedwick directs Sharon Smyth and David Henesy in rehearsal while associate director Sean Dhu Sullivan looks on.

1968: Grayson Hall arriving to work.
1969: Jonathan Frid with the day's script.

1970: Lara Parker and David Selby at a script reading.

"Wait a beat before you sink your fangs into her neck!"

"Turn your head on the pillow—all we're getting is nostrils!"

"Drop that speech about the lights—you'll be carrying a candle!"

In the early days, Bob Costello usually had a pronunciation note for me because, he insisted, I had a funny Minnesota way of saying words like doll, hover, water and roof.

We were blessed with excellent directors and I learned much from all of them. Besides Lela and Henry, there was John Sedwick and Jack Sullivan (aka Sean Dhu Sullivan) With only minutes to spare before taping, the notes came in a verbal shorthand, with Henry's comments always the most choice. Lela instinctively knew how to give everyone that little something extra to go for, so we wouldn't settle in. With all the special effects and only one chance for a clean take, how tempting it was to play it safe. Yet the most inspired and satisfying moments always happened when things went desperately wrong and one had to rely on wit and instinct to put things right. *Dark Shadows* provided plenty of challenging opportunities.

One day, before appearing in a scene with Joan Bennett and Grayson Hall, I had to make a costume change on the run from another set at the far end of the studio. As I trotted up to the grand entrance of Collinwood, the stage manager grabbed my arm and whispered urgently that Joan and Grayson, who were already playing the scene, lacked the necessary props—a letter and a small revolver. I grabbed them, tucked them in my muff, made my entrance, and surreptitiously distributed them during the course of the scene. We never stopped during the air show. In those days, editing was too expensive. But working "live" was exciting and I came to love it.

A lamp smashed one day not three feet from where Josette sat writing a letter and I never flinched. Sarah's dress got caught on a branch in the woods and, hilariously, the actress managed to uproot a tree and drag it along throughout the rest of the scene. During a dramatic moment in a cemetery, Angelique almost tipped over a styrofoam gravestone with a gentle swish of her cape. Drafts blew out candles. Secret panels sometimes needed an extra shove to open magically. The gusts blowing on Widows' Hill sometimes required a firm grip on veils and wigs. All *Dark Shadows* actors have stories about such mishaps as door knobs that fell off with a single twist, fangs that snapped in half, and brandy decanters with stoppers that wouldn't unstop. These were daily occurrences that kept us alert, tested our nerves and added to the fun. There wasn't a single day during the four years I appeared on *Dark Shadows* that I didn't look forward to going to work. I loved every minute I spent in Studio 16.

Maggie Evans had a couple of "Pops"—two different actors who played Sam Evans, an alcoholic artist living in a cluttered shanty studio by the sea. That set, by the way, was my favorite, but once Maggie became a governess at Collinwood, it disappeared along with the diner set. Mark Allen originated the role, and then David Ford took over. Both actors who played Pop had difficulties remembering lines and relied heavily on the TelePrompTer. Toward the end of his days in the show, the second Pop became blind, which necessitated wearing dark glasses, the better for the actor to read the TelePrompTer undetected.

Finally the episode came when Maggie stood at Pop's hospital bedside, his death at hand. Ross Skipper, the big red-headed cameraman, wheeled in closer and struck his camera base on the end of the hospital bed causing the TelePrompTer to fall off and crash to the floor. Pop sat bolt upright in bed and hollered, "Where is it?" Maggie just reached out a firm hand, gripped his shoulder and shoved him back against the pillows, saying, "Never mind, Pop. It's going to be okay." Pop expired without saying another word.

1968: JONATHAN FRID AS BARNABAS COLLINS AND GRAYSON HALL AS DR. JULIA HOFFMAN.

Dark Shadows will forever be known for the "bloopers." Yes, dead bodies blinked and ghosts did not always materialize on cue. It's true, one could frequently see crazed terror in the eyes of an actor who'd completely forgotten his lines and couldn't find any appropriate words on the TelePrompTer. A wayward prop man was seen "on air" walking into the Old House basement. During the end credits, Barnabas was seen gathering up his wardrobe and ambling off the set. Attacks of sneezing, coughing and stuttering can happen to anyone, even ghosts and witches. Certainly, even vampires have to swat away at pesky flies flitting about dark, dank crypts.

I remember visiting my family in Minneapolis years after *Dark Shadows* was off the air and watching an old rerun. I howled with laughter when I saw a scene between Grayson and me, both of us dolled up in wigs and veils reading an old manuscript by candlelight with a foam-covered microphone dangling over our heads.

I will only offer an explanation, not an apology. Somehow, between the hours of 8:00 a.m. and 3:45 p.m., we taped a daily half-hour show five times a week. This wasn't a "kaffe klatch" show where all we had to remember was to steer clear of end tables and not bump into the sofa. We had new sets every day and, thanks to the skill and imagination of Sy Tomashoff, five acres of woods with a creepy cemetery and a treacherous cliff were crammed into five square feet of studio space. Technicians new to the show arrived with only hours to perfect complicated special effects. We all pitched in to make it work and when it didn't, I'd like to think it helped make the show more endearing.

It was Lara Parker as Angelique who had the nasty job of fixing curses on people by sticking pins into dolls, hypnotizing the unsuspecting into performing dreadful deeds, and delivering long incantations to spark fires that would consume her enemies. It meant that Lara was always confronted with perilous special effects and the prospect that they'd foul up. During one episode, she had an especially long incantation to deliver while staring at a pile of carefully arranged playing cards that were supposed to burst into flame. This scene was intercut with scenes of Vicki and the effect of this conflagration in her room. There was a lengthy commercial break before Lara's scene started and an overly eager prop man popped in repeatedly to add "just another spritz" of lighter fluid to ensure that the pile of cards would burn on cue. Unfortunately, they blazed in one terrific "whoomph" long before Lara had a chance to finish her long-winded incantation. She was left to work her magic over the charred remains.

ANGELIQUE IN THE 1970
PARALLEL TIME STORYLINE.

As actors on *Dark Shadows* we dealt with candles that wouldn't stay lit and glass chimneys that toppled off kerosene lamps, but edits were made only in very rare instances. Once Jonathan was so irritated with his performance that he uttered a four-letter word to force a reshoot. Who else among us would have dared resort to such a tactic, other than our beloved and very popular star vampire! We were often heartsick and mortified that we couldn't redo a particular scene, but we lived with it. It's easy to blank on another character's name, but I recall a particular show when I couldn't seem to say even my own name without stumbling. I defy anyone to figure out what or who I was talking about in that episode. When it was over, I was almost in tears, but I knew there would be no chance of redoing the segment.

There were only a few times over the run of *Dark Shadows* when we had to redo a complete show. On one occasion, one of my favorite actors left the studio after morning rehearsal and decided to imbibe, rather than eat his breakfast. When Bob Costello finally located him wandering in the neighborhood and returned him to the studio, it was clear to everyone that he was in no condition to play a scene with Maggie in the diner. Less than a minute into taping, we all heard Lela's voice over the loudspeaker in the control room telling us to return Sunday morning to tape the show!

I'm sure I walked through thirty miles of cobwebby corridors (shrouded in vapors from endless pots of dry ice) calling "Willie, where are you? Help me! Please, please come to me, Barnabas!" There were days when our camera rehearsals were entirely devoted to special effects and we simply skipped over the dialogue to get to the next gag. We all worked entirely in the moment, concentrating on remembering lines we'd barely rehearsed. To this day, I remember individual moments but cannot recollect the progression of a single story line. I'm mystified when a fan writes to ask me about a particular plot.

I dearly wish I could have eavesdropped on a few writers' sessions. It's my guess that one of them had suffered a bad experience with an unwelcome British houseguest. How is it that a visiting cousin or friend from England always turned out to be a vampire, a gold digger or some other nefarious creature? It's clear that our writers took full advantage of the opportunities for satire and social comment. Eve, the man-made mate created for Adam, sprang to life fully formed mentally and physically, and simply despised the fellow at first sight. The writers also took potshots at religious and moral precepts whenever they dealt with the hypocritical and avaricious Reverend Trask or one of his descendants. Casting

1968:
BARNABAS AND VICTORIA WINTERS (ALEXANDRA
MOLTKE); BARNABAS AND JULIA (GRAYSON
HALL); WILLIE LOOMIS (JOHN KARLEN) AND
BARNABAS (JONATHAN FRID).

1897: David Selby as
Quentin Collins.

matinee-idol-handsome and devilishly charming Humbert Allen Astredo to portray Nicholas Blair, Satan's emissary, was certainly an amusing comment on hell.

The writers always kept us in the dark about the plot lines, except to tease us with cryptic hints. Shortly before I got the first Lady Kitty Hampshire script, Sam Hall said to me, "Better brush up on your English accents, my dear." We seldom got scripts more than a day or two before rehearsal, yet our schedules were posted several weeks in advance. More than one actor looked up in panic from a read-through rehearsal to ask "Hey, am I going to die or something?" We never knew.

I remember Dan Curtis vowing never again to plot a story line that took place before telephones were invented; I think because it meant hiring more actors to serve as messengers to deliver handwritten notes. We had quite a history of introducing actors who spent weeks on the show without speaking. David Selby and Terry Crawford as the ghosts of Quentin Collins and Beth Chavez, were probably the first to appear as mute characters. Jim Storm was also silent for ages before he finally got a few words to speak.

Kate Jackson was hired to play Daphne while she was still a student at the American Academy of Dramatic Arts. The Academy had a policy that forbid students from accepting professional employment before completing the two-year course. Dan called the Academy's registrar and told him not to kick her out because she wouldn't be speaking. He was as good as his word and she was mute for months. Like Josette, many characters appeared first as ghosts, apparitions and werewolves while their roles in the storyline were developed.

Normally, we finished taping at 3:45, then grabbed a cup of coffee to watch the "air show" which came on at four o'clock. Those who were in the following day's episode assembled around the big table in the rehearsal room for a read-through of the new script. Changes were made, scenes discussed and then we were on our feet for a preliminary blocking. At 6:00 p.m. we wrapped for the day.

The Brittany du Soir was our local watering hole, a pub-like French restaurant on the corner at Ninth Avenue. Most of us gathered there at the end of the day—cast, crew, staff, and often Dan Curtis with the writers. We

1840: KATE JACKSON AS DAPHNE HARRIDGE.

1968: HUMBERT ALLEN ASTREDO AS NICHOLAS BLAIR, ROBERT RODAN AS ADAM, LARA PARKER AS CASSANDRA, ALIAS ANGELIQUE, AND JONATHAN FRID AS BARNABAS.

were a friendly lot and enjoyed being together. I can't remember the first time I was asked for an autograph or when I noticed that the small groups of fans waiting outside the studio had grown into a mob. Since I'd been with the show from the beginning, the growth in popularity seemed gradual and I took it in stride.

After Jonathan Frid joined the show and created the iconic character of Barnabas Collins, *Dark Shadows* became a huge success. Yet, in the beginning, the cast members greeted the introduction of the vampire on April 17, 1967 with some trepidation. Our reactions ranged from "You gotta be kidding!" to "Give me a break." I don't think anyone was particularly pleased at the turn of events. An afternoon horror melodrama with ghosts and goblins did not sound like a class act. But Jonathan cared about his work and was determined to create a real and believable character. And Jonathan was delightful. He was soft-spoken, almost courtly in manner and especially polite. It's not easy for anyone to walk into an established show without a tremor of nerves and apprehension, but his assignment was more fraught than most.

Maggie first encountered Barnabas Collins when he appeared at the Collinsport Diner, complete with cape, wolf's-head cane and knuckle-duster-sized ring. Several of the actors stood around in the diner set, arms folded, staring dumbly as Jonathan modeled his costume and discussed, with utmost seriousness, his ideas about the ring and cane. We all pondered whether or not he should have an accent. In the end, he made the role of Barnabas Collins uniquely his own.

KATHRYN LEIGH SCOTT AS A DISFIGURED JOSETTE DUPRES.

The complexity of the character was intriguing. Barnabas was essentially evil at first, but one felt sorry for him because, poor man, he suffered the fearful guilt and loathing of his curse: in order for him to survive, others must die. His love for Josette was eternally doomed and he was a despised wretch who, at times, wielded immense supernatural powers and, at other times, was an impotent creature lying helplessly chained in a coffin. One responded to this sad-eyed despair with the romantic notion of saving him from himself.

The situations were often absurd, but we played everything with intense seriousness. On one level, the horrifying events were so terrifying that angry letters arrived at the studio complaining that the show caused young children to have nightmares. But we received just as many letters from doctors, lawyers, nurses, teachers and students who found *Dark Shadows* hilarious and a welcome half-hour break in the day. We also got some mail that was pretty far out. It was the '60s and one can only speculate on the substances some members of our audience may have used to enhance their viewing pleasure.

One lunchtime I dropped by the studio to pick up some scripts and check my schedule. I found Bob Costello and June wrestling with a clothes dummy

JONATHAN FRID IN HIS 1795 BARNABAS COSTUME.
JERRY LACY AS REVEREND TRASK IN 1795.
KATHRYN IN HER 1795 JOSETTE COSTUME.

draped in veils and an antique-lace dress. The idea was that this dummy, properly lit and photographed, would appear as a ghostly apparition named Josette. No matter what they did, it looked like a dummy draped in tatty cloth. I offered my two-cents' worth of advice and was rewarded with Bob's offer to dress me up in the gown and let me stand-in for the dummy.

I backed off at first and then got caught up in the fun. It meant greasing my hair down with baby oil, then powdering it with talcum powder.

"What happened to this woman?" l asked.

"She jumped to her death off Widows' Hill," I was told.

I was positioned in front of the camera in a greenish light, and a fan blew against my face causing my eye to tear up and weep. Poor Josette! I was practically sobbing and couldn't help myself. I lifted my weary arms, as instructed, opened my mouth and soundlessly entreated my lover to "come to me, come to me. . ." I was there for hours having a wonderful time.

In a later episode when Josette's ravaged ghostly presence appeared, Vinnie Loscalzo designed a gruesome makeup—a ping-pong ball painted like an eye and glued to my cheekbone with my own eye covered in putty and grease paint. The worse he made me look, the worse I wanted to look. The more battered and bloody the better, I thought. I wanted my hair dripping like seaweed around my face and more bloody gashes around my bruised and blackened eye.

A couple of actors thought I was crazy to volunteer for "extra" work and asked if I was getting paid for it. So I asked Bob if I was getting paid for it. No, he said, it wasn't a regular show for me. I wasn't going to be paid at all? He didn't think so. After all, they could still use the dummy.

I continued to play the ghost of Josette for no pay, and "volunteered" to do her scream as well. They'd hired a girl to do the scream, but it was a weak-kneed, elegant little sound that infuriated Lela. It had no guts. Lela asked me to scream and I let out a blood curdling roof-raiser that pleased her. I screamed for no pay, too.

In general, we were not overpaid on *Dark Shadows*.

A large oil portrait of Josette in happier days had appeared over the Old House mantel and she looked a lot like me. It was a subtle transition, but eventually I beat out the dummy and finally became the official Josette—and got paid for it.

Josette DuPrés was a young, naive girl, who arrived in Collinsport from a plantation in the island of Martinique with her father, André, and her maid, Angelique Bouchard. Lara and I had a great time together babbling French at each other as Josette and Angelique. That lasted only one episode before our appalling French accents were scrapped.

The first Josette dress was a low-cut, high-waisted Empire style in white and pink chiffon with puffy, little-girl sleeves. That dress, plus a wig with huge sausage curls nestled around my chubby cheeks, made me look like an acre of pink cotton candy. Josette DuPrés, in appearance and character, could not have been more different from Maggie Evans.

All of us wondered if it wouldn't be confusing to the audience to have me play two entirely different, unrelated characters. Could we get away with it? We did, and to great effect. Dan never stopped experimenting and, once Josette was established, we moved back in time, and other actors on the show assumed various 1790s roles. From then on, we functioned like a stock company, each with our own repertoire of characters.

Mitch Ryan, Alexandra Moltke and Joel Crothers eventually left the show, while Grayson Hall, Lara Parker, Jerry Lacy, John Karlen, Dennis Patrick, James Storm, Clarice Blackburn, Christopher Pennock, Marie Wallace and David Selby joined the cast.

Most people identify Jerry Lacy with his fantastic impersonation of Humphrey Bogart, while I immediately think of him as the irascible, fire-and-brimstone preacher. Reverend Trask. And Willie—what would Barnabas have done without Willie Loomis to release him out of his coffin every night? I'll always remember Willie's plaintive, wheedling voice and his old tweed jacket. I figured Willie for the sort who'd eat mice in the stable if he got hungry. Clarice, with us almost from the beginning, was our own

1968: Roger Davis as Jeff Clark and Kathryn as Maggie Evans

Mrs. Danvers. It was a revelation to watch this gifted actress develop her multi-layered characterization of Collinwood's housekeeper, Mrs. Johnson.

Dennis Patrick (whose shameful limericks will not be quoted here) walks away with the *Dark Shadows* award for best-loved, funniest and, certainly longest, death scene: an agonizing demise by some sort of horrible Leviathan creature. It's said that hysteria reigned in the control room, with everyone screaming, "Die, Dennis, die!" But to no avail. As Dennis quivered, staggered and gasped through death's agonizing final throes, the stage manager flapped his arms and signaled desperately to the still writhing actor to wrap it up.

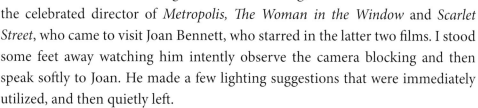

1897:
DAVID HENESY AS JAMISON COLLINS.

We had a number of distinguished guests visit the *Dark Shadows* set. Among them was Fritz Lang, the celebrated director of *Metropolis, The Woman in the Window* and *Scarlet Street*, who came to visit Joan Bennett, who starred in the latter two films. I stood some feet away watching him intently observe the camera blocking and then speak softly to Joan. He made a few lighting suggestions that were immediately utilized, and then quietly left.

After finishing another show, I tore up the stairs and stopped dead in my tracks.

There was Gale Sondergaard, who'd just watched the taping in the upstairs Green Room. "That was a very nice job," she said to me. "You reminded me of the roles I used to play when I was your age." I grinned with pleasure and thanked her very much. She had been among Hollywood's Black Listed and had not worked as an actress for many years. I'm sure she was at the studio for an audition, and I would have loved to see her join our company.

Roger Davis showed up one afternoon with his new girl friend, a nineteen-year-old Texas beauty named Ellen. She'd arrived in Manhattan only weeks before to embark on a modeling career and eagerly showed us her portfolio. Her beauty was staggering—and we happily assured Roger that Ellen, who used the professional name, Jaclyn Smith, had a good chance of making it as a model. As the romance blossomed, she visited the studio frequently and soon Roger announced their engagement.

HOUSE OF DARK SHADOWS: DAN CURTIS
DIRECTS JONATHAN FRID AND KATHRYN
LEIGH SCOTT IN THE 1970 FEATURE FILM BASED
ON THE ORIGINAL TELEVISION SERIES.

We also worked with many child actors, though none of them were ever treated like children After we watched one little girl work her way flawlessly through a scene Grayson whispered, "Forty, if she's a day." They were always word perfect—"They have to be, they can't read the TelePrompTer"—but sometimes they didn't move to the right place at the right time . . . "so, they're small, shove 'em."

In fact, they were no trouble at all and no one ever felt the need to make concessions to them just because they were kids. David Henesy was on the show from the very beginning and I adored him. He was the same age as my brother David and the resemblance between them was remarkable: the same sandy hair, brown eyes and shy smile. Don't kids get cranky sometimes? Don't they whine and fidget? Not these kids, who managed to be normal children and professional actors at the same time.

There'd been talk off and on about a *Dark Shadows* movie, but no one took it seriously until we all drove up to Tarrytown one morning and actually started filming at the old Jay Gould estate. Sam Hall and Gordon Russell had written a script, which none of us had read, and we knew that Dan Curtis would direct it. He'd already directed several episodes of the series. We knew he dreamed of making the feature film, but the reality of doing so seemed so remote.

Dan encouraged a very supportive, family atmosphere, often taking huge crowds of us out to dinner and organizing other social gatherings. He was always around and obviously cared about all of us. In turn, I think we all felt a responsibility and intense loyalty to him. We wanted to help him get this film off the ground. But there were difficulties. On one occasion he rounded up a group of us who had roles in the film and took us with him to a meeting with a major independent producer who'd expressed interest in financing the film. The producer declined and we all went to a sidewalk bar afterward to discuss the next step.

Finally, Dan got his financing and we were set to roll. The logistics of juggling actors schedules must have been a nightmare since the series continued taping while the film was being made. Some of us with larger film roles were written out of the series for several weeks, but others worked both on location in Tarrytown and in Studio 16.

1970: DONNA WANDREY AS ROXANNE DREW, A NEW LOVE INTEREST FOR JONATHAN FRID'S BARNABAS.

On the first day of rehearsal for the film, Dan gathered us together in the kitchen of the huge estate for "a talk." He told us about the miniscule budget, tight schedule and his hopes for the film. He could do it, he said, only if we pitched in and gave him our complete cooperation. That meant the pay was low, the hours long, and that we would be roughing it. It was an exhilarating pep talk and we may have applauded at the end. I hope so.

I remember very little of the actual filming. It passed in a blur. But each day in the car on the way back to Manhattan, I stared out the window and replayed each scene, knowing too late how I should have done it. Well, it was Dan's first film, too. Maybe he was feeling the same way.

By the time we finished filming *House of Dark Shadows*, my contract had expired. I continued working on the series while deciding what to do next. After I returned to Manhattan following a publicity tour for *House of Dark Shadows* I told my agent I'd decided to leave the series. Then I called Dan from the studio pay phone after I'd finished taping a show. "Are you all right?" he asked. "You sound funny. You better get over here so I can talk to you."

I walked cross-town to Dan's office on Madison Avenue, thinking about what I would say. I knew I would leave the show, but I was torn. Dan and I had a long heart-to-heart talk that day that I will always cherish. I left *Dark Shadows* grateful and proud of the four years I'd spent working with such a wonderful cast and crew, and ready to move on to new adventures.

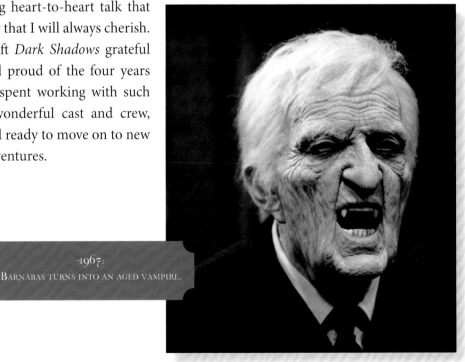

1967:
BARNABAS TURNS INTO AN AGED VAMPIRE.

Angelique
Looks
Back

By
LARA PARKER

FOR SOME OF US IT WAS OUR FIRST PROFESSIONAL JOB—AN AFTERNOON SOAP OPERA THAT WAS GOTHIC ROMANCE, A SUPERNATURAL COSTUME DRAMA, AN OVER-THE-TOP THEATRICAL PASTICHE, AND A CELEBRATION of the imagination, all wrapped up in the story of a tortured vampire. We did not know it at the time, but those of us who were actors on the original *Dark Shadows* series back in 1966 through 1971 were given a special legacy; we were part of the creative team that produced an enduring classic, a show that inspired thirty years of re-runs, as well as DVDs, fan conventions, numerous remakes and imitations. Today we are surrounded by vampire stories; *Dark Shadows* was the first which offered something richer and deeper.

And so, when Johnny Depp and Tim Burton decided to make a film based on our show, it seemed like the icing on the cake. It was dizzying to contemplate such powerful Hollywood involvement in something we produced almost forty years ago when we were all very young and very inexperienced. But they were not the only audience members to have experienced that deep connection. In fact, hundreds if not thousands of fans have told us that in their formative years they used to rush home from school to watch *Dark Shadows*, and that in many ways the series changed their lives. We have grown to think of our show as something rare and original, and to appreciate the cult following it has acquired. Many of us have faithfully attended the yearly conventions to meet hundreds of new fans, and some of us even published books based on the series. Nevertheless, the prospect of a Burton/Depp production was incredibly validating.

However, as time passed, the making of the film began to seem like the stuff of fantasy. The talk had been floating around for years, and nothing had happened. A script was written, and then another. Meanwhile, conventions came and went and we had no answers for our eager fans. Even when announcements of a start date were made in the press, it was hard to take them seriously, mostly because we had been waiting so long. For these reasons it was a shock to receive a phone call on a Thursday evening in June that I was to fly to London the following week to do a cameo in the movie along with fellow original series alumni Jonathan Frid, Kathryn Leigh Scott and David Selby.

Even when I was settled into my first class seat on Air New Zealand, I still felt as though I were floating in a fairy tale. I found it hard to believe that I was to be in a Warner Bros picture inspired by *Dark Shadows* starring an impressive list of actors, and that giant sets were being constructed for the film on one of the most celebrated movie lots in the world.

At Pinewood Studios, just outside of London, we were fitted for our costumes the first afternoon and then received a tour the next day. Johnny Depp and

LARA WITH DAVID SELBY ON THE OUTSIDE BACKLOT.

Tim Burton were on the set filming and we were introduced all around. Johnny Depp remained in character and we saw him made up as the vampire for the first time. His face was whiter, his black hair had lengthier, curvier spikes, and his long, yellow nails were more lethal than our Jonathan's had been, but he looked very handsome—a young, rakish Barnabas with a devilish smile.

There was an unforgettable moment when the two Barnabases were talking face to face that I would have photographed for posterity: the two profiles, Johnny and Jonathon, one older, grey and slightly jowly, the other younger, black-haired and finely chiseled. It was a picture I took with my mind.

Johnny was extremely kind to Jonathan and even said to him, "None of us would be here if it weren't for you." I looked around at the magnificent set and felt extremely proud.

Tim Burton uses a smoke machine when he films to produce a haze through which the colored spotlights create blue and red and green rays. The effect is magical, as if the air were full of rainbows, and the sets look like impressionistic paintings. Rather out of place at Collinwood, but wonderful all the same time, were glass cages high above the floor where go-go dancers in silver metallic briefs and boots gyrated to the music. Ah, the '70s.

Our moment before the cameras was brief. The four of us, Jonathan, David, Kathryn and I, arrived and walked through the front door of Collinwood. We paused and greeted Johnny Depp in his splendid Barnabas makeup before descending the stairs. David Selby looked very handsome in his '70s make-up with gray sideburns and a silver medallion, but Jonathan was a bit disoriented. I'm sure it was overwhelming for him. It was so much grander than our studios back on 53rd street in New York City.

After the take, Tim Burton introduced us to the cast and crew. "This is the original cast from the *Dark Shadows* series," he said, and we received generous applause.

Even though it was mind boggling to walk on the set created for *Dark Shadows*, it was the brief encounters with the cast members that I will never forget. After Kathryn finally convinced an overly solicitous assistant director that we did not want to stay in our dressing rooms, we were allowed to sit backstage behind the monitors and watch the day's filming. There were over a hundred extras in a great variety of '70s costumes—psychedelic patterns on the dresses and mod boy suits.

Helena Bonham Carter, playing Julia Hoffman, came dancing by in an orange wig saying she had overslept and would come and visit with us after she completed her scene. At first I failed to recognize her, but then I thought, Julia Hoffman, of course—red hair! We watched on the monitor while she filmed a scene at the party in which she had no lines, only a long moment where she was slightly inebriated and was also going a little mad. A dozen different subtle emotions floated over her angelic face. Finally, tired of the take, she reached up and drew a finger across her throat, meaning "Cut!" Only the director can call, "Cut," but I guess being Tim Burton's partner and the mother of his children gave her a little extra clout on the set.

After her scene she came backstage and chatted with us for at least an hour while we stared, fascinated by her adorable get up, not only the orange flip wig but a frothy dress with a tiny bodice and a short, full skirt. Not like the Julia Hoffman we used to know!

She admitted that when Tim told her they were doing *Dark Shadows*, she had said, "I'll have the role of Angelique, thank you very much!" She later revealed that she loved playing Julia and that she had never played an alcoholic psychiatrist before. She said the whole cast was watching our show on DVDs in the make-up room, and what's more, they were all hooked! However, she didn't mention, as she did in a later interview, that she thought our soap opera had been "hilariously bad."

Michelle Pfeiffer, playing Elizabeth Collins, came out to meet us and to pose for pictures. She was cool and a bit detached, perfectly made-up and coiffed, and so fragile, she almost seemed as if she might break. She wore a diaphanous dress of many shades of blue, and her hair was teased into a bouffant. She was gracious, the perfect *Dark Shadows* matriarch, and so beautiful; I don't think I have ever seen a tinier waist.

We had a moment with her on camera where Kathryn, David and I were meant to be improvising party chatter just before she turned and looked disapprovingly at her daughter, Carolyn, up on stage with Alice Cooper. One of the plot points, as in the original series, was that Elizabeth was a recluse and had not left Collinwood for fourteen years. We did the take several times and each time one of us ad-libbed something—never to be heard over the music of course.

Sitting backstage watching the monitors beside Alice Cooper was as entertaining as it gets, listening to him talk about his career and his family in his signature ghostly make up—his eyes thickly rimmed in black, with long black spikes painted through them and black lines pulling down the corners of his mouth.

I knew he was perfect for the *Dark Shadows* movie, when he performed his next song writhing in a straight jacket. A true Gothic, shock-rock entertainer, he sometimes brought a bloody guillotine and an electric chair on stage. He did, however, deny that he had ever bitten the head off a chicken, a rumor that had made him famous.

He told me at the beginning of his career as a musician, he had looked around and noticed that all the successful singers were wholesome, pretty boys with smooth vocals; he decided to go 180 degrees in the other direction, He said, "I saw a lot of rock heroes and I thought, why not a rock villain? Murderous and bloody, with vampire make-up!" It was the '70s, the time of peace and love, and he said, "We drove a stake through the heart of the Love Generation." Right on!

But the high point for me was meeting Eva Green who was playing Angelique. I had watched her in *Camelot* on HBO and I thought she was a marvelous choice—gorgeous, but also compelling and passionate. She had already accumulated an impressive resumé, working in a James Bond movie and also a film directed by Burtolucci. In interviews, she claimed that in acting school in Paris, she had always chosen evil roles, even Lady Macbeth!

She came back stage to say hello with her blond wig wrapped up in a huge net made of sparkly gold webbing. We spoke for a while and she confided in me saying that the role of Angelique was for her an amazing gift. "The part is multi-layered," she added.

I felt a pang of melancholy. I realized that I had a proprietary feeling about the character of Angelique. Five years of playing the part, twenty years of syndications all over the world, and over thirty years of attending *Dark Shadows* conventions had led me to assume that the role of Angelique would always be mine alone. Yes, there had been remakes, but later actresses had played her as a sexy, one-dimensional villainess. I always saw her as more complex, and I wondered whether Eva Green would discover those deeper levels she spoke of.

I was a stage actress before I went to New York, and I played many leading ladies in college theater and summer stock. I always saw myself in the role of the heroine, (preferably the princess!). Playing the villain felt unfamiliar and uncomfortable until one day in rehearsal Jonathan Frid said to me, "Stop suffering and

LARA PARKER AT THE WITCH MUSEUM IN SALEM, MASSACHUSETTS WHILE CONDUCTING RESEARCH FOR HER *DARK SHADOWS* NOVEL *THE SALEM BRANCH*.

stop crying. You are not the victim. You're the heavy! You have the plum role, so you might as well enjoy it.

I had to grow into the role of Angelique. I had to find deep within myself the authority to play her powerful moments. Even though Jonathan was right and his advice was good, I think that if at that point I had changed my process and made Angelique into nothing but a cold-hearted witch, the subtleties in her character would have been lost as well as the impression she made on those watching at home.

Even though she could be vicious and cruel—and fans loved her for that— I never thought that Angelique was born evil. I believe they also identified with Angelique's struggle, and the fact that she never gave up hope. Every time she was

·1968: ANGELIQUE (LARA PARKER), RISEN AS A VAMPIRE, TAUNTS BARNABAS (JONATHAN FRID).

discouraged, every time Barnabas rejected her, she came back and pledged her love again. She always believed that in some way she would find a way to make him desire her. And, paradoxically, as my playing of Angelique evolved, she became stronger—and yes, she did become meaner—but she also became more sympathetic. Ironically, she became the heroine I always wanted her to be.

When Eva Green told me that the part of Angelique had many layers, I hoped that she saw her underlying vulnerability, and the never diminished belief that she would finally find a way to win Barnabas's heart. Someone who was pure evil would have given up long ago and only sought revenge. Angelique wanted desperately to be loved.

Perhaps my analysis of Angelique was deepened in writing three novels that featured her, along with many other *Dark Shadows* characters, in original stories.

In all three books Angelique has awesome powers and is capable of dastardly deeds. But she also fights adversity and struggles to overcome heartbreak.

In the first novel, *Angelique's Descent*, I tried to explain her everlasting devotion to Barnabas by going back to her childhood in Martinique and telling the story of her first betrayal by her adopted father. I wanted to delve into the character of a child who had been deceived by someone she loved, and see what kinds of scars that would leave.

She wanted so desperately to be seen as the person she was, to be appreciated and respected. But her station in life had made her feel unworthy, and she had to constantly fight feelings of inadequacy. Every time she rose to a moment of power it was a victory over the harsh world around her. But it was also a victory over herself.

In *The Salem Branch*, I decided to explore the story of a character I played in only one episode, that of Miranda du Val, a young woman tried for witchcraft in 1692 during the Salem witch trials. I saw her as the first incarnation of Angelique, a true witch with powers she tried to hide in a threatening environment, powers that were thrilling and deeply moral but forbidden in a Puritan society.

In my third novel, in order to escape the devil's clutches Angelique has split herself into two persons, Antoinette and Jacqueline, mother and daughter, both inexplicably drawn to Barnabas. I have explored the concept of duality, how two personalities can reside in one. The werewolf is the best example, going back to *Dr. Jekyll and Mr. Hyde* portraying the good and the evil sides of one man; or *The Picture of Dorian Gray,* the story of a charismatic young man whose dark persona resides in a hidden portrait. Which of the two is he really?

Or is he in some way both? Just as our vampire on *Dark Shadows* was both a hero and a monster. Even as a vampire, he experienced guilt and remorse. For me, this duality, this two-sides-to-every-character was the most fascinating aspect of Angelique. She was cruel, yes, and seemed to have a heart of stone, but the fires inside her were ignited by a determined struggle to win the heart of her beloved and claim her place in the world.

———— ✥ ————

And so, folded into my album of memories is another *Dark Shadows* chapter. The trip to London and to Pinewood studios was a never-to-be-forgotten experience for me, but a tribute as well to a unique television series which aired so many years ago.

I have the feeling that the movie will be different from our show in many ways. There will be incredible special effects that will take our breath away and put to shame our dry ice fog and chroma key disappearing acts. There will be no missed lines or microphones dangling in the shot. And although we were often (unintentionally) funny, we were always genuine. This time there will be sly efforts at farce.

ANGELIQUE AS A VAMPIRE.

LARA AS A GHOSTLY ANGELIQUE IN
NIGHT OF DARK SHADOWS

Our Barnabas—though sometimes a bat—never slept hanging upside down from the chandelier.

Nevertheless, for some reason our show continues to haunt and seduce those who ran home from school to watch it, as well as the thousands of fans who came along later. It will be interesting to see what the Tim Burton/Johnny Depp version brings to the mix. I have a suspicion that they too will become unexpectedly mesmerized and will fall—along with their enviable resources—under the magical spell of *Dark Shadows* once again.

The Mansion on the Hill

David Selby on the *Dark Shadows*
television set o the Collinwood foyer,
patterned after Seaview Terrace.

By

KATHRYN LEIGH SCOTT

ON A SPARKLING, UNSEASONABLY WARM LATE OCTOBER AFTERNOON, I STOOD ON THE BLUFFS IN FRONT OF SEAVIEW TERRACE, AS IT'S KNOWN BY LOCALS IN NEWPORT, RHODE ISLAND, AND LOOKED AT waves crashing against a rocky shore. Yes, *those* waves, the ones that made their debut more than 45 years ago under the opening credits of the premiere episode of *Dark Shadows*. I couldn't stop myself from humming the opening bars of Robert Cobert's famous theme music and recalling those wistful words spoken by the young governess, Victoria Winters . . . *My journey is beginning . . . a journey to link my past with my future . . .* on her way to the mysterious Collins Mansion.

EDSON BRADLEY ESTATE, NEWPORT, RHODE ISLAND

But what I was experiencing in nature's glorious technicolor, we in early 1966 viewed in grainy shades of gray, lending even more ghostly shadows to the mansion on the hill with the haunting glow of light in a single upstairs window. And therein lies a story I was to discover in October 1999 as a guest author attending *Haunted Newport* Hallowe'en celebrations.

Seaview Terrace, also now known as the Carey Mansion, had been built in the 1920s for a wealthy Washington D.C. distiller (producer of Old Crow whisky) who requested that his architect, Howard Greenley, pattern the summer home after a particular chateau in France. The family stayed in their vacation house with the ocean view only about three times. As often happened after the Great Depression and the introduction of federal income taxes during the 1930s, the wealthy owners could no longer afford the luxury of the huge household staffs necessary to the upkeep of these lavish summer homes that were not built for year-round living. The house had not been inhabited for a decade prior to World War II when Seaview Terrace was used as barracks for naval personnel. Windows were broken and the lawns overgrown when the mansion was purchased for back taxes in 1949 and converted for use as a summer school called Burnham-by-the-Sea.

SEAVIEW TERRACE INTERIOR

In early May of 1966, Dan Curtis arrived in Newport with his set designer, Sy Tomashoff, to scout exterior locations for ABC's new afternoon soap, *Dark Shadows*. The Gothic architecture of Seaview Terrace had caught Tomashoff's discerning eye as a suitably brooding facade for the Collins mansion which was set in the mythical town of Collinsport, Maine. Curtis negotiated to film the opening credits at Seaview Terrace for the sum of $500, with the owner's stipulation that filming would have to be completed before school opened in late June. However, to the consternation of the school's staff, Dan Curtis arrived unannounced with a film crew at noon the day before the summer term was to begin. The crew set up their cameras and spent the afternoon filming on the grounds of Burnham-by the-Sea. By late afternoon, the weary headmaster asked if they were finally finished shooting. No, Curtis told him, they would also be shooting that night and would need to have the entire mansion dark except for one light shining in a window. The headmaster protested that with school beginning in the morning, he had a lot of work to do and needed the lights on. After considerable persuasion

SEAVIEW TERRACE INTERIOR

ALEXANDRA MOLTKE ON THE CLIFF
AT SEAVIEW AS DAN CURTIS
AN FILM CREW PREPARE TO SHOOT
BELOW IN 1966.

(Curtis, after all, had a television series to launch!) the schoolmaster was relegated to a room in the turret where he worked by candlelight with a blanket covering the window.

Curtis returned one more time to film on the grounds of the school, where Alexandra Moltka, Louis Edmonds, David Henesy and, later, Thayer David, were seen in exterior scenes. Beginning in 1976, the mansion housed Salve Regina University dorm and classrooms for three decades.

That October evening in 1999, after a lecture and book signing, my hosts introduced me to The Black Pearl on Bannister's Wharf. Not only is the charming restaurant and tavern famous for its New England chowder, but, with its rustic black lacquer interior and red-checkered tablecloths, it's easily recognizable to any *Dark Shadows* fan as the exterior used for the show's Blue Whale tavern. The very long, very narrow building is about 100 years old and was originally used as a rigging shop in the days when the only way to get off the island was by ship. During the winter months, the ships would dock at Bannister's Wharf and the masts would be hauled into the shop for repairs. The rigging shop was converted into a restaurant in the early 1960s. The wharf area was once known as Blood Alley, a rough neighborhood with colorful strip joints and bars that catered to

Kathryn Leigh Scott and Jonathan Frid make visits to Seaview Terrace ("Collinwood").

sailors and fisherman—and certainly would have lured "Pop," Maggie's dear old dad, Sam Evans. I can picture him, sketchpad in hand, roaming the waterfront and then nipping into the Blue Whale for a convivial whisky with Bob the bartender. Today the wharf is a quaint promenade with restaurants, shops and galleries. As we strolled the moonlit wharf after a wonderful meal at the Black Pearl, I couldn't help but imagine myself as the young Maggie Evans walking hand-in-hand with Joe Haskell after a hamburger and a dance or two at the Blue Whale. Once again, as I looked out over the water at the bobbing sailboats, I found myself humming a few bars of Robert Cobert's nostalgic Blue Whale music and remembering my good friend Joel Crothers.

Surely somewhere in this evocative setting, lurking in the dark shadows of the wharf, Barnabas Collins was watching us, a sinister gleam in his eye.

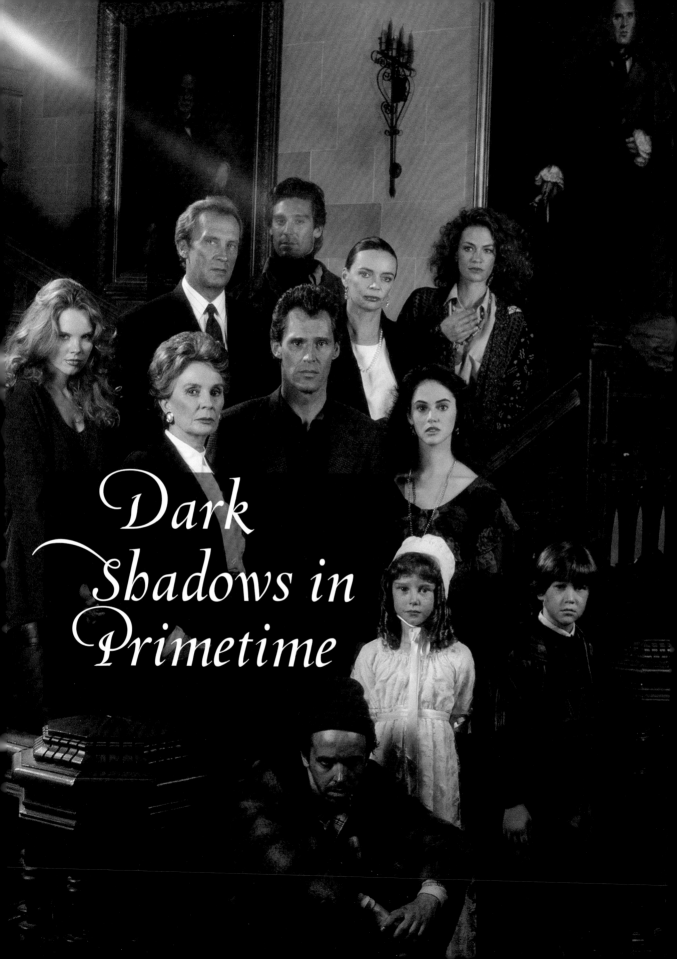

Dark Shadows in Primetime

PREVIOUS PAGE PHOTOGRAPH: 1991 *DARK SHADOWS* CAST, CLOCKWISE FROM LEFT:
BARBARA BLACKBURN (CAROLYN STODDARD), ROY THINNES (ROGER COLLINS),
BEN CROSS (BARNABAS COLLINS), MICHAEL T. WEISS (JOE HASKELL), BARBARA STEELE
(DR. JULIA HOFFMAN), ELY POUGET (MAGGIE EVANS), JOANNA GOING (VICTORIA WINTERS),
JOSEPH GORDON-LEVITT (DAVID COLLINS), VERONICA LAUREN (SARAH COLLINS), JIM FYFE
(WILLIE LOOMIS) AND JEAN SIMMONS (ELIZABETH COLLINS STODDARD).

By
JIM PIERSON

*I*N LATE 1989, PREPARATIONS BEGAN FOR A REINCARNATION OF *DARK SHAD-OWS* TO BE PRODUCED FOR THE NBC-TV NETWORK BY DAN CURTIS PRO-DUCTIONS IN ASSOCIATION WITH METRO-GOLDWYN-MAYER TELEVISION. Commissioned by NBC president Brandon Tartikoff, this revival would mark *Dark Shadows'* debut as a weekly nighttime series, although it would use the original daytime series as a foundation for its stories. In fact, the primetime adaptation was very much a remake that also integrated elements from the 1970 feature film *House of Dark Shadows.*

Unlike the original daytime *Dark Shadows*, which was produced in a small Manhattan ABC-TV studio on a limited 1960s soap opera budget, the 1990s version would have much larger financial resources to enhance and expand the show's look. With the two-hour pilot budgeted at $4 million—and the subsequent hour episodes running $1.2 million each—the return of *Dark Shadows* could afford numerous luxuries never dreamed of for the 1960s serial. Series creator-executive producer-director Dan Curtis gleefully declared that the rebirth of *Dark Shadows* would have the resources to be the show that original fans recalled from their youth, but bigger and scarier.

The casting would also be grand, with Oscar-nominated film actress Jean Simmons stepping into the Elizabeth Collins Stoddard role that earlier movie queen Joan Bennett had occupied in the original show. Veteran television star Roy Thinnes (*The Invaders*) would inherit the role of brother Roger Collins and actress Barbara Steele, a favorite star of cult Italian '60s horror films, who had served as a producer to Curtis on his acclaimed mini-series *The Winds of War* and *War & Remembrance*, was enlisted as the new Dr. Julia Hoffman, confidant to guilt-ridden vampire Barnabas Collins, who would be portrayed by British actor Ben Cross (*Chariots of Fire*). Up-and-coming actress Joanna Going, who was then known for her work on the daytime serial *Another World*, was hired in the pivotal dual role of governess Victoria Winter and Barnabas' ill-fated fiancé Josette DuPrés.

On Monday, March 19, 1990 at 11:00 a.m., filming began on the pilot. With Curtis at the helm, the crew set up at Gulls' Way in Malibu to shoot the first scenes: Sheriff George Patterson (Michael Cavanaugh) visiting Professor Michael Woodard (Stefan Gierasch) at Woodard's seaside cottage. After a full inaugural day, including an afternoon at Paradise Cove, the *Dark Shadows* company relocated to the Trancas Restaurant & Nightclub in Malibu, which would serve as the Three Gables Roadhouse. But, most importantly, the Trancas parking lot would be the location where, after sundown, Barnabas Collins would emerge after twenty years.

That first night of filming would test the vulnerable vampire's stamina. Ben Cross, the new Barnabas, arrived for make-up at 4:00 p.m.; he was scheduled to

1991: BARNABAS (BEN CROSS) ATTACKS A STRANGER (HOPE NORTH).

report to the set two hours later. His scenes with Gloria (Hope North) and Muscles (Michael Buice) were to commence after dark. But with the inevitable first-day delays, Barnabas did not go before the cameras until the midnight hour, and filming continued in chilly temperatures until 3:30 the next morning. Television's most famous vampire was back in fittingly haunting fashion.

After two more days of location filming in the greater Los Angeles area, the *Dark Shadows* cast and crew settled into what would be their home for both the pilot and the subsequent series—the Greystone estate in Beverly Hills.

A majestic Tudor-style mansion built in the late 1920s by millionaire oilman Edward Doheny, Greystone sits on eighteen hillside acres of land accentuated by formal gardens. The 55-room structure has been featured in numerous television and film projects over the decades. Since 1965, it has been owned by the city of Beverly Hills, which began operating the historic landmark as a public park in 1971.

Greystone woud serve as the exterior of the ominous Collinwood estate as well as most of the Collinwood interiors, with the exception of the foyer, great hall and drawing room. Sets for those would be specially built on Stage 6 at the Warner Hollywood Studios.

In a case of filmmaking trickery, Greystone would also function as the Old House exterior (from the front side only), and all of the Old House interiors with the exception of Barnabas' bedroom, which would be constructed on Stage 6. Other areas of the Greystone property to be seen in the pilot and series would be the stables, abandoned swimming pool (which had actually been filled-in by cement years prior) and the multiple levels of gardens.

An area of the Greystone basement was used to create the sheriff's office, Barnabas' cellar coffin room, and jail cells for the 1790 story. The building adjacent to the greenhouse was transformed into Maggie Evans' (Ely Pouget) studio apartment. Large production trucks, vans and trailers were set up in the parking lot at Greystone to house equipment, wardrobe and dressing rooms. The normally vacant interior of the mansion was filled with antiques and other furnishings specifically as props for *Dark Shadows*. The mystical aura was complete once park rangers began to educate the cast and crew regarding Greystone's tortured past, including tales of alleged haunting and mysterious death.

Although *Dark Shadows* had taken over virtually all of Greystone, the estate remained open to the public during regular park hours, 10:00 a.m. until 5:00 p.m. During that time, the crew kept filming in roped off and guarded areas in an effort to keep curious visitors from interfering with the production. Since the public is not allowed inside the mansion—except on special occasions—the interior filming was less problematic.

To create the illusion that a Beverly Hills mansion surrounded by palm trees was really an eighteenth-century New England estate overlooking the Atlantic Ocean, an elaborately detailed miniature of Greystone was designed and constructed for use on *Dark Shadows*. As with the real Greystone, the miniature would represent both Collinwood and the Old House, which would eventually be somewhat confusing to viewers. But, unlike the actual Greystone, the miniature would be situated on a dark, jagged cliff at the edge of the ocean. Additionally, the miniature would feature made-up sections of Greystone that did not exist in reality.

Under the expertise of special effects artist Bill Millar, the miniature was constructed at a cost of approximately thirty-five thousand dollars. It was not actually built until the fall of 1990, months after the pilot was completed and *Dark Shadows* had been picked up as series by NBC. Actually the word miniature is not the most

1991 *DARK SHADOWS* SERIES BUMPER TITLE CARD WITH MINIATURE OF COLLINWOOD.

accurate description for the elaborate model that Millar and his team came up with, which measured twenty-five feet along the front and fifteen feet deep.

One special effect that was, literally, hard to swallow, was the smoke used on the set to give scenes a moody, hazy appearance. Upon being exposed to the airborne mineral-oil based fog for endless hours, cast members found it uncomfortable, if not unhealthy, to breathe. Unlike the crew members, they could not wear protective breathing masks. After vigorous complaining, the offending mixture was replaced with an oil-free solution.

On April 5, 1990, the fourteenth day of filming the pilot, the production moved to Warner Hollywood Studios Stage 7, home of the basketball court-sized interior of the Collins Mausoleum and secret room. This would be the day for recreating handyman Willie Loomis' fateful unleashing of Barnabas from his two centuries-long imprisonment in a chained coffin.

The next morning, the company travelled to the woods of Fern Dell at Griffith Park to shoot exteriors intended to represent the cemetery surrounding the mausoleum. For the subsequent series filming, the simulated graveyard would be situated on the front grounds at Greystone, while the mausoleum and secret room interior set would be relocated in Greystone's parking lot.

The fourth, and final, week of filming the pilot marked the unveiling of the majestic Collinwood foyer, great hall and drawing room sets, designed by Fred Harpman, on Warner Hollywood's Stage 6. The cavernous great hall, two stories in height with an upstairs corridor, represented one of the largest, most elaborate and costliest sets every constructed for a television pilot, let alone for a series. With each section sporting four solid walls and a ceiling, being on the set gave the cast, crew and visitors the feeling that they were really inside a genuine Gothic mansion.

After eighteen days of production, filming of the pilot wrapped on Wednesday, April 11, 1990. Over the ensuing four weeks, Dan Curtis and his post-production team assembled a preliminary cut of the pilot to submit to NBC for consideration as a series in the coming 1990-1991 television season. On May 16, the initial edit of the pilot was delivered to the network so that Tartikoff and his colleagues could view the completed project and decide if they felt the effort should be picked up as a new series for the NBC fall schedule.

It would be a week before NBC officially announced their line-up for the 1990-1991 season, but with the tremendous amount of publicity surrounding *Dark Shadows'* resurrection, the audition of the pilot appeared to be just a formality. Yet, when the NBC revealed their schedule, *Dark Shadows* was nowhere to be found.

Dan Curtis received an apologetic phone call from Tartikoff, who explained that *Dark Shadows* had narrowly missed getting greenlit. But the ever-tenacious Curtis wasn't prepared to give up without a fight. He expressed his shock and dismay to Tartikoff, pointing out that there had been an understanding from the beginning that the show was destined to get on the air. Within days, Tartikoff responded with an offer for five new *Dark Shadows* episodes to be put on NBC's schedule as a mid-season replacement. However, Curtis knew the abbreviated order was half-hearted as well as inadequate for a show of *Dark Shadows*' format and scope. It simply wouldn't be financially sound for Curtis and MGM to produce a minimum of five episodes. The expense and ambition of the show would require a commitment of at least thirteen hours. But Tartikoff declined and Curtis notified the stunned cast and production members that Barnabas would not be rising from the dead as planned.

However, in the grand tradition of the melodramatic formula that is at the core of *Dark Shadows*, two days later Tartikoff phoned Curtis with a reprieve; NBC had reconsidered and was now prepared to offer a firm thirteen-hour order for *Dark Shadows* to start airing early in 1991. Tartikoff promised that the series would be given priority back-up status, assuring that it would be inserted into the schedule as soon as an opening became available.

By midsummer of 1990 when the series would go into production, nearly three months had passed since the pilot had been completed. Most of the crew members had gone on to other projects but several key personnel would return to participate in the series. Since NBC ordered thirteen hours of the show, eleven additional hours, comprising episodes 2 through 12, were now to be produced to follow the two-hour pilot episode. Curtis and Supervising Producer Steve Feke moved swiftly to assemble a full production team. Matthew Hall, son of original series actress Grayson Hall (Dr. Julia Hoffman) and his father Sam Hall, a writer on the original series, returned as writers after serving as technical advisor and creative consultant duties, respectively, on the pilot. Among the new recruits to be part of the writing staff were Jon Boorstin, M.M. Shelly Moore, Linda Campanelli and William Gray.

An innovative production schedule was devised for *Dark Shadows* when it resumed filming on July 23, 1990, at Ports O'Call and Fisherman's Wharf in San Pedro, California. These waterfront areas would serve as settings for the village of Collinsport. Multiple episodes were shot simultaneously to help curb high production costs. Curtis would continue to direct episodes 2, 3 and 4. Armand Mastroianni took the reigns for episodes 5 and 6 with Paul Lynch handling episodes 7 and 8, Rob Bowman on episodes 9 and 10 and Mark Sobel finishing out with episodes 11 and 12.

In mapping out the storyline for episodes 2 through 12, Curtis and his writing staff continued to adapt the original series' major plots into a new framework. Recalling the immense popularity of the daytime version's flashback sequences, Curtis determined that the 1990s *Dark Shadows* would also delve into Barnabas' past, revealing how he became a vampire. Starting with episode 7, the original 1795 storyline would be reworked, set in 1790, focusing on the cursing of Barnabas by the beautifully wicked witch Angelique (Lysette Anthony).

LYSETTE ANTHONY AS ANGELIQUE.

THE GREYSTONE MANSION AS
THE OLD HOUSE.

Unlike the 1960s *Dark Shadows*, the new incarnation would not feature entire episodes set in the past. NBC had been strongly opposed to the show utilizing any period stories that would place the show in a costume drama approach. As a compromise, Curtis structured episodes 7-12 of the 1991 series to contain scenes set both in the past with the Collins family ancestors and in the present with the modern day characters.

Once production on the final six episodes was well underway, it became apparent that the elaborate requirements of the 1790s segments were placing a serious strain on *Dark Shadows*' already sizeable budget. The extra time required for the special costumes, hair styling and set dressings meant added production time and expense. In an effort to avoid further cost overages, MGM informed Curtis that all scenes in the remaining episodes must be shot at Greystone, with the exception of the Collinwood interiors and Barnabas' bedroom sets that remained on the Warner Hollywood sound stages.

As a result, series set designer Bryan Ryman and his staff were faced with the challenge of adapting and disguising areas of Greystone to serve as completely new locations. Although a genuine ocean cliff had served as Widows' Hill in the third episode, in episode 9 the location would have to be created on the

Greystone grounds. This was accomplished by constructing an artificial rock formation, made of fliberglass, along the hillside adjacent to the driveway leading to Greystone's parking lot. Utilizing wind machines, strategic camera angles and stock ocean footage, it appeared as if Jeremiah (Adrian Paul) jumped off an actual cliff into the sea. The design staff's ingenuity was also reflected in the transformation of the Old House drawing room into the Collinsport courtroom interior for episode 11. Following these successful efforts, designer Ryman figured he could create virtually anything at Greystone.

Following a four-day Thanksgiving weekend break, *Dark Shadows* began its final days of filming during the first week in December. The practice of alternating the stories between the present time and the eighteenth century within the same episode had led to production delays. Although originally scheduled to finish filming on November 26, episodes 11 and 12 lingered before the cameras until December 5. To help finally bring production to a close, both Dan Curtis and Armand Mastroianni returned to direct with a second production unit while Mark Sobel completed directing other scenes. Among the scenes shot on the final day were retakes of the courtroom sequences under Curtis' direction.

On the night of December 5, a wrap party was held at the El Paso Cantina Restaurant & Bar in Hollywood. Most of the cast and production members joined together to celebrate the end of filming, anxiously anticipating the series' broadcast debut, which was scheduled for the following month.

A massive publicity campaign began immediately. NBC aired promotional teaser spots starting in mid-December, alerting viewers to the January, 1991, debut of *Dark Shadows*. A nationwide radio contest with the theme "Don't Be Afraid of the Dark" was conducted nationwide, offering prizes such as original *Dark Shadows* videotapes and custom miniature wooden coffins. Grand prize winners were flown to Los Angeles for an advance screening of the pilot and a party. NBC enlisted Domino's Pizza as a promotional partner and their innovative marketing techniques also included the placement of theatrical style trailers for the show on monitors in United Artist movie theaters as well as Circuit City and Highland electronic stores across the country.

On Sunday, January 6, a press conference with Dan Curtis, Ben Cross and Jean Simmons was held at the Ritz-Carlton Hotel in Marina Del Rey, California, as part of NBC's annual press tour. The nation's journalists were given a preview of the four-hour "mini-series" and the opportunity to interview the three representatives from the show. A press party with additional cast members was held that evening at Greystone.

Special "sneak-preview" screenings were held in Los Angeles, New York and Chicago during the first week of January, 1991. NBC further hyped *Dark Shadows'* premiere by scheduling the two-hour pilot for Sunday, January 13, with episodes 2 and 3 placed back-to-back the following night. The network promoted these first four hours as a mini-series, with the actual weekly series hours to begin in a regular Friday night time period the same week. As a result, five hours of the new show would be seen in the course of just five days.

When the pilot aired, it came in a solid second place in overall household ratings for the time period, receiving a 14.6 rating and 23 percent share of the audience. But most significantly, it was the highest rated show in its time period

JOANNA GOING AS VICTORIA WINTERS AND BEN CROSS AS BARNABAS.

for the most desirable audience demographic categories, including women ages 18 to 34 and 25 to 54 as well as men in the same categories. The show was also number one among teens and kids.

The critics' reviews were mostly favorable and it was instantly apparent that the new *Dark Shadows* had won over not only the apprehensive original series followers, but also a whole new legion of devotees. In addition to countless newspaper articles—back when newspapers were still the main source of information—features on the return of *Dark Shadows* appeared on numerous television magazine shows (*Entetainment Tonight, Inside Edition, The Today Show, Live With Regis & Kathie Lee*) and prominent publications (*Newsweek, TV Guide, People, Entertainment Weekly*).

Monday, January 14, the second night—comprising episodes 2 and 3—of the mini-series style roll-out of *Dark Shadows* also yielded encouraging results. But in a matter of days, an untimely international incident would inflict a fatal wound.

By the time the first regular hour-long presentation of *Dark Shadows*—episode 4—appeared on Friday, January 18, the Gulf War had begun and television network programming had been heavily disrupted for the previous two days. NBC chose to delay *Dark Shadows* one hour past its scheduled 9:00—10:00 p.m. Pacific Time airing so that the network's highly successful Thursday night block of comedies could be shown on Friday after being preempted the previous night. Because the schedule changes were all made at the last minute, printed television logs—back in the days before the Internet—did not reflect the actual schedule. As a result, confused viewers tuned in to see *Dark Shadows* but found *Cheers* instead. Causing further damage was the fact that the episode only aired that night in the Eastern and Central Time zones when NBC pre-empted it in the Pacific and Mountain Time zone for a news special on the Gulf War crisis.

The following Friday, January 25, NBC attempted to salvage the situation in the West Coast markets by scheduling the unseen episode 4 back-to-back with the week's new episode 5. But the harm had already been done. *Dark Shadows'* momentum had been interrupted by the war and the timing could not have been worse.

On March 8, NBC moved *Dark Shadows'* Friday night time slot an hour later to 10:00 p.m. Eastern and Pacific times in the hope of building the audience for the final three episodes of the season. Even though the show had maintained a strong audience in the 18-49 age category, the ratings had fallen with the erratic scheduling and not as many older viewers were watching. NBC had been partially to blame with their ill-advised emphasis on promoting the horror aspects of *Dark Shadows* instead of its more commercially accessible romantic appeal, which has always made the show particularly popular with women of all ages.

When final episode 12 aired on March 22, an increase of nearly one million viewers had tuned in from the previous month since *Dark Shadows* began airing later on Friday nights. Given the ongoing strength of the program's draw with the advertiser-friendly demographic, the chances for a second season renewal were looking hopeful. Curtis and the writers outlined story ideas for the start of year two.

1790 STORYLINE:
BEN CROSS AS BARNABAS AND
JIM FYFE AS BEN LOOMIS.

Aware that the *Dark Shadows* revival was in danger of extinction, the nationwide network of fans quickly banded together to voice their undying support. NBC headquarters in Burbank, California and New York were flooded with calls and letters requesting *Dark Shadows'* renewal, a tactic that had recently worked for another NBC cult favorite *Quantum Leap*. The campaign to save *Dark Shadows* reportedly equaled the 50,000 pieces of mail that the *Quantum Leap* effort had generated. Fans also organized rallies with picket signs at NBC affiliates in eighteen cities on May 8, 1991—designated as "Save *Dark Shadows* Day." At the Burbank, California gathering, series actors Roy Thinnes (Roger Collins), Michael T. Weiss (Joe Haskell), Ely Pouget (Maggie Evans), Lysette Anthony (Angelique) and Joseph Gordon-Levitt (David Collins) dropped by to demonstrate support and thank the fans.

The incredible outcry generated considerable press coverage. However, bad luck emerged once more when Brandon Tartikoff decided to depart NBC for Paramount Pictures. His successor Warren Littlefield chose to clean house by cancelling *Dark Shadows* and bringing on more new shows that would reflect his own programming strategies. Ironically, a few years later Warren Littlefield contacted Dan Curtis to admit that based on *Dark Shadows'* desirable audience demographics and its growth potential he had made a mistake canceling the revival. With the impending loss of the Danielle Steel television movie franchise, Littlefield asked Curtis if he would be willing to bring *Dark Shadows* back as a series of occasional two or four-hour productions. Unfortunately, Curtis explained that a large ensemble cast such as that used for *Dark Shadows* could not easily or affordably be available when needed, unlike the Columbo telefilms which only required the scheduling and availability of one actor. Secondarily, Curtis also had doubts that the serialized nature of *Dark Shadows* would lend itself to infrequent, scattered airings many months apart.

Upon disappearing from NBC, the thirteen hours of the 1991 *Dark Shadows* were repeated on the Sci-Fi Channel several times and sold in several foreign countries. Videotapes were issued with additional, unaired footage, outtakes and bloopers. T-shirts, model kits, wrist watches, posters, comics and a commemorative book were issued as well, ironically all emerging after the show was cancelled.

Despite its all-too short life, the 1991 *Dark Shadows* revival clearly reinforced the devotion of the original fans and made a lasting impact on millions of first-time viewers who became part of a new generation of faithful followers that would continue to keep the legend of *Dark Shadows* undead.

JOANNA GOING (VICTORIA WINTERS), JOSEPH GORDON-LEVITT (DAVID COLLINS), BARBARA BLACKBURN (CAROLYN STODDARD), BEN CROSS (BARNABAS COLLINS), ROY THINNES (ROGER COLLINS).

ROY THINNES (ROGER COLLINS), JEAN SIMMONS (ELIZABETH COLLINS STODDARD), WAYNE TIPPIT (DR. FISHER), JULIANNA MCCARTHY (MRS. JOHNSON), BARBARA STEELE (DR. JULIA HOFFMAN)

1994: BARNABAS AND VICTORIA

1994: Barnabas and Dr. Julia Hoffman

1994:
Daphne's funeral;
Joe Haskell.

1991: Barnabas and Carolyn

1790 STORYLINE:
BEN CROSS AS BARNABAS, JOANNA GOING AS
JOSETTE DUPRESS AND THE FUNERAL OF JEREMIAH.

1790 STORYLINE:
Barnabas, Abigail (Julianna McCarthy) and Naomi Collins (Jean Simmons), Natalie DuPres (Barbara Steele) and Reverend Trask (Roy Thinnes).

Hidden
in the
Shadows

PREVIOUS PAGE:
Dark Shadows 2004 pilot: Ivana Milicevic as
Angelique, Alec Newman as Barnabas Collins and
Marley Shelton as Victoria Winters.

Above: Marley Shelton as Victoria, Alexander Gould
as David Collins and Matt Czuchry as Willie Loomis.

By

JIM PIERSON

WHEN THE *DARK SHADOWS* PRIMETIME SERIES FOR NBC ENDED AFTER ITS TWELVE-EPISODE RUN IN MARCH OF 1991, DAN CURTIS KNEW THAT THE PROPERTY REMAINED EXTREMELY VALUABLE AND that it had not been given a fair shot by the network after the Gulf War had disrupted its scheduling.

In 1992, the Si-Fi cable channel debuted nationwide. The outlet's first program purchase was all 1,225 episodes of the 1966-71 series, which would remain on the service for the next decade, primarily based on its success in bringing female viewers to Si-Fi. This new outlet provided helpful exposure, keeping the *Dark Shadows* franchise visible on a significant level.

By the summer of 1993, Curtis and William Gray—who had served as a writer, script editor and co-producer on the NBC effort—collaborated on a script for a proposed *Dark Shadows* feature. The film would again reprise the familiar story from the previous television incarnations in which governess Victoria Winters arrives at Collinwood to look after troubled young David Collins, and drifter/handyman Willie Loomis unwittingly releases vampire Barnabas Collins from his chained coffin after two centuries of imprisonment. The latter incident had also been a key plot point in the 1970 M-G-M motion picture *House of Dark Shadows*—mostly a condensation of the original Barnabas storyline as seen on the *Dark Shadows* daytime series in 1967. Curtis and Gray further integrated *House of Dark Shadows* elements into the new movie script after having adapted much of the earlier film's story into the 1991 series. The script was eventually submitted to several studios for consideration—with Miramax Films briefly expressing interest—but with the recent perceived failure of the NBC series, the timing was apparently not right to re-launch *Dark Shadows* again so soon.

Curtis remained committed to resurrecting *Dark Shadows*. Another opportunity arose in 1997 when 20th Century Fox's television production arm—called Twentieth Television at the time—and The Fremantle Corporation proposed producing with Curtis either a new daytime version or a weekly primetime version. A daily version in the original soap opera format was preferable since the Fox Network was considering possibly expanding their affiliate programming into the daytime market—a scenario that did not transpire. For the next four years, Fremantle continued to explore possibilities to resurrect *Dark Shadows* as a syndicated primetime weekly hour-long series but the deal was contingent on filming in Canada for budgetary reasons, a stipulation that Curtis could not accept as he felt the program would need to be produced under his watchful eye in Los Angeles, close to home.

In 1998, NBC-TV chief Warren Littlefield told Curtis that the network had cancelled the 1991 primetime series prematurely and expressed interest in returning *Dark Shadows* to NBC in the form of occasional television movies. Curtis quickly vetoed that format, feeling that the serialized nature of *Dark Shadows* would not lend itself to just a few installments each season. In fact, keeping a large cast together on an irregular basis would be extremely difficult. Curtis brought in writer Manny Coto to collaborate on scripts for a new NBC-TV primetime series, as well as developing an outline for an entire first season. As with the previous

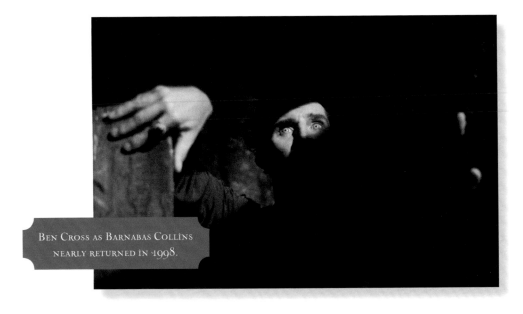

BEN CROSS AS BARNABAS COLLINS NEARLY RETURNED IN 1998.

efforts to relaunch *Dark Shadows*, the basic introductory elements of the original tale were present with plans to expand into new territory as the series progressed. It was also hoped that most members of the 1991 series would return. However, NBC ultimately passed and *Dark Shadows* was again left in limbo.

For his next *Dark Shadows* reincarnation attempt in 2000, Curtis turned to the theatre world. His old friend Pierre Cosette had enjoyed great success producing *The Will Rogers Follies* on Broadway, and there was also the recent popularity of *Dr. Jekyll & Mr. Hyde* and other high-concept, genre vehicles on stage. Dan Curtis Productions' vice-president David Kennedy suggested that *Dark Shadows* could have the same impact. Research disclosed that Tony Award-winning composer Rupert Holmes (*The Mystery of Edwin Drood*) was a fan of the series. When contacted, Holmes jumped at the chance to work with Curtis on the story, and soon travelled from New York to Los Angeles to begin collaborating. Original music composer Bob Cobert was engaged to create the songs with Holmes as lyricist. After a week working together, Curtis was elated. He even felt confident that he could direct a Broadway production for the first time, despite no experience in that medium. Sadly, Holmes was unable to follow up on the project due to personal matters and the *Dark Shadows* musical became another victim in a long string of unrealized ambitions.

In 2001, Curtis teamed with Aaron Spelling's company, Spelling Television, in an attempt to bring *Dark Shadows* to the Fox Network as a primetime weekly serial. Writer Eric Bernt was hired to pen the story with new twists, including introducing the character of Angelique in the premiere episode. Curtis' creative input remained a vital element but in early 2002, after delivery of Bernt's script, Fox decided not to pick up the project.

Also in 2001, Fremantle made one last attempt to get in the *Dark Shadows* business with a plan to produce a new daytime version in Spanish using the original daytime series' scripts. But the idea once more failed to materialize.

A short time later, the TNT network expressed interest in airing a possible weekly *Dark Shadows* series. On a different note, an animation studio met with Curtis to discuss a possible animated *Dark Shadows* for adults that could potentially air on HBO or another cable television channel and perhaps use voices of the original series' actors. An animated version never materialized.

In 2002, Curtis again looked into the possibility of *Dark Shadows* becoming a theatrical motion picture but the timing didn't seem right.

Finally, in 2003, Curtis received word that the company headed by producer John Wells, of *ER* and *West Wing* fame, was interested in putting together a new *Dark Shadows* series that would air on the Warner Brothers WB network. Once business matters were nailed down, writer Mark Verheiden was brought in to work with Curtis in creating the script for a one-hour *Dark Shadows* series pilot. Verheiden had been the show-runner for the WB *Smallville* series that centered on the life of Superman as a young man. A fan of the original *Dark Shadows*, Verheiden brought a fresh perspective to Curtis' penchant for reworking the familiar narrative that propelled the previous *Dark Shadows* productions.

With a one-hour pilot, the decision was made to streamline the story by not incorporating all of the *Dark Shadows* characters. The plot would focus on the Collins family and, with some new twists, on developments surrounding the arrival in Collinwood of Victoria and Barnabas. Among the most dramatic touches was the introduction of Angelique, the witch, giving the pilot a stronger dose of tension and excitement.

Casting the 2004 *Dark Shadows* pilot proved to be extremely challenging since the show would be produced by Curtis and Wells for Warner Brothers, who would license it to the WB network. Meetings with the WB revealed certain casting expectations that were not in line with what Curtis and the other producers envisioned. Finally, it was decided that relatively unknown British actor Alec Newman would inherit the role of Barnabas Collins and rising star Marley Shelton would take on the role of Victoria Winters, playing her as a blonde for the first time.

Additional cast members included Blair Brown as Elizabeth Collins Stoddard, Martin Donovan as Roger Collins, Alexander Gould as David Collins, Jessica Chastain as Carolyn Stoddard, Matt Czuchry as Willie Loomis, Jason Shaw as Joe Haskell, Kelly Hu as Dr. Julia Hoffman and Ivana Milicevic as Angelique.

Rob Bowman, who had directed a pair of the 1991 *Dark Shadows* episodes before going on to helm the *X-Files* television series and films, was hired to direct the pilot. Bowman, Curtis and the producers scouted locations at the Greystone estate in Beverly Hills, which had been Collinwood in the 1991 version and would again represent the ominous home of the mysterious Collins family, albeit with modern digital effects to give the exterior a grander, gloomier presence.

It was announced that *Dark Shadows* would serve as the replacement for another popular vampire series, *Angel* (a spin-off of *Buffy The Vampire Slayer*),

2004 *Dark Shadows* pilot:
Barnabas (Alec Newman) and
Victoria (Marley Shelton)

on the WB. The network began making lavish promotional plans to launch *Dark Shadows* in the fall of 2004. Unfortunately, the latest endeavor to bring back Barnabas was doomed before a frame of film was shot.

Principal photography was set to commence promptly, allowing for completing and editing of the pilot in time for the announcement of fall series pickups by the network in May.

With less than a month before commencement of shooting, Rob Bowman backed out of his commitment when he was offered directing chores on a feature film project. With no one else readily available whom he trusted, Curtis decided that he would direct the *Dark Shadows* pilot. However, the youth-centric WB network immediately objected to the change, insisting they wanted a younger navigator with a fresher, quirkier style than Curtis' more traditional approach, a situation that marked the beginning of the end of Curtis' participation in the project.

After lengthy, heated discussion between Curtis, Wells and the WB, Australian director P.J. Hogan (*My Best Friend's Wedding, Muriel's Wedding*) was secured to direct the *Dark Shadows* 2004 pilot. Unacquainted with *Dark Shadows*, Hogan's seeming lack of respect for Curtis' vision and the subject matter caused an immediate rift, prompting Curtis to effectively walk away from any further involvement. Hogan was then left to steer much of the pilot into a direction that fatally compromised the pilot's sure-fire chances of being picked up as a series.

The 14-day filming of the pilot began on Friday, April 2, 2004—thirty-three years to the day when the original *Dark Shadows* aired its last daytime episode on ABC-TV—back at the Greystone estate with exterior and interior settings for Collinwood.

The crew then moved to the historic and long-shuttered Los Angeles Theatre in downtown Los Angeles. The 1931 Baroque-style gilden interior with set dressing, including dozens of burning candles, was used to represent the Old House foyer and hallways as well as the rooms of Barnabas and Josette. The dilapidated mansion's exterior and surrounding woods would be created with green screen special effects in post-production.

Next came all-night shooting at The Sable Ranch in Canyon Country outside of Los Angeles, the locations for the Collins mausoleum, cemetery and woods exteriors. The Warner Brothers Studios soundstages in Burbank would be home to sets for the mausoleum interior, Willie's room and the interior of the train in which Victoria would take her fateful ride to Collinsport.

DARK SHADOWS 2004 PILOT:

TOP ROW: ALEC NEWMAN AS BARNABAS COLLINS, MARLEY SHELTON AS
VICTORIA WINTERS, MARTIN DONOVAN AS ROGER COLLINS.

MIDDLE ROW: BLAIR BROWN AS ELIZABETH COLLINS STODDARD,
MATT CZUCHRY AS WILLIE LOOMIS, JESSICA CHASTAIN AS CAROLYN STODDARD.

BOTTOM ROW: IVANA MILICEVIC AS ANGELIQUE, ALEXANDER GOULD AS
DAVID COLLINS, KELLY HU AS DR. JULIA HOFFMAN.

As with the 1991 show, Ports O' Call in San Pedro would serve as an exterior portion of Collinsport, this time as the train station where Victoria arrives, as well as home to Joe's fishing boat at the town's waterfront.

Production on the pilot ran behind, forcing Hogan to forego shooting one of the key scenes in the script. A rough edit was hastily assembled without full special effects. A temporary music score was implemented from the Warner Brothers music library, drawing on such films as *The Shining*.

It had been evident during the filming and the viewing of daily production footage that P.J. Hogan's *Dark Shadows* pilot had veered away from the show's established blend of Gothic romance and horror. His campy version concluded with a screaming match between Victoria and Angelique that resembled a send-up skit on *Saturday Night Live*.

Despite the pilot's underperformance, it was still hoped the WB would retain enough interest and faith to allow *Dark Shadows* to become a primetime series. Salvage attempts centered on shooting additional scenes, reshooting others and recasting some of the roles. In fact, there had been disagreement at the WB over the casting of Newman as Barnabas. Some executives had wanted a more traditionally handsome actor in the "soap stud" mold. Such a concession had already been made with the hiring of Matt Czuchry as Willie, a major contrast from the manic portrayal in the 1991 series in which Jim Fyfe's seedy appearance included rotting teeth.

The failure of the 2004 pilot of *Dark Shadows* became a textbook case of how mishandling and interference can doom even the most promising of creative enterprises. In this case, it was a $4 million dollar blunder that Warner Brothers could not recoup. Unlike the 1991 primetime *Dark Shadows*, which began as a 90-minute pilot—with an additional 13 minutes of outtake scenes—the 2004 incarnation ran barely over 40 minutes and could not be broadcast as a movie or special because of its short length, abrupt ending and lack of finished special effects or music. The whole enterprise remains a disjointed reject buried in the Warner Brothers vaults with no feasible reason to exhume it, other than for morbid curiosity.

It should be said, however, that the pilot offered several promising performances, especially those of Marley Shelton as Victoria and Alec Newman as Barnabas. Additionally, Alexander Gould proved himself a solid young actor as the mischievous juvenile, David, and future *Weeds* co-star Martin Donovan displayed an appropriate arch portrayal of his stern father, Roger. Although Jessica Chastain had limited screen time as Carolyn in the pilot, in a few years she would become a heralded screen actress in such films as The Help and The Tree of Life.

The following year, ABC-TV expressed interest in a weekly *Dark Shadows* series before deciding on a remake, ironically, of *The Night Stalker* series focusing on journalist Karl Kolchak and his encounters with the supernatural. Curtis had produced the original *Night Stalker* TV movie in 1972, one of the highest-rated small-screen films of all time. He was hired as consultant on the short-lived 2005 series.

Dan Curtis was able to end his long and illustrious career on a high-note with a pair of prestigious television films, *Saving Milly* and *Our Fathers* in 2005. Prior to his death the next year, initial discussions with Johnny Depp's representatives had begun to take place regarding Depp's interest in bringing back *Dark Shadows*—and vampire Barnabas Collins—to a whole new audience.

DAN CURTIS ON THE SET OF THE 1991 *DARK SHADOWS* PRIMETIME SERIES.

HOUSE OF DARK SHADOWS:
CAROLYN STODDARD (NANCY BARRETT)
RISES AS A VAMPIRE.

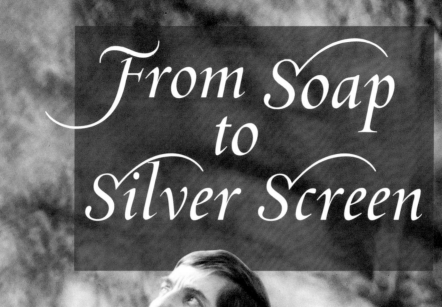

From Soap
to
Silver Screen

By
KATHRYN LEIGH SCOTT

Among my happiest memories of *Dark Shadow* were big family-style get-togethers that Dan Curtis would organize on the spur-of-the-moment, usually after an ABC-TV media reception or public relations event. On these rare and wonderful occasions, Dan would round up his brood and herd us into a nearby restaurant. On one memorable evening Dan confronted a restaurant manager with: "Whad'ya mean you're closing the kitchen? We're here, aren't we?" The manager was helpless in the face of Dan's forceful presence (and his inimical scowling grin that even Jack Nicholson would envy), and we simply took over the restaurant. Actors, writers and assorted *Dark Shadows* staff members pitched in to help the waiters shove tables together and find enough chairs. In minutes we were assembled at a long table, a boisterous, tight-knit, crazy-quilt family enjoying a night out.

It may have been that very night that Dan first floated the notion that we might make a movie together. No two people could be less alike than Dan Curtis and Mickey Rooney, but the spunk of Andy Hardy and "Hey, guys, let's get together and put a show on in the barn . . ." has a certain resonance when you realize that, eventually, the *Dark Shadows* movies were MGM productions. And in that great spirit of "we'll show Hollywood" camaraderie, we all rallied around Dan to help him "put on his show." Never mind that no one had ever before spun a soap opera off into a movie, or that *Dark Shadows* had no "hiatus" in which to shoot a big-screen version on location. If Dan could pull it off, we would be taping a daily half-hour series in the studio while simultaneously filming somewhere in the hinterlands.

The veteran actors in our company—Joan Bennett, Grayson Hall, Louis Edmonds, Thayer David and Dennis Patrick—certainly knew the ropes, but the young ones considered the whole enterprise a lark. Once he had a script, written by Sam Hall and Gordon Russell, Dan enlisted various cast members to accompany him to meet "money people." I remember being one of the rag-tag contingent Dan took with him to a meeting with famous independent film producer Joe Levine. I had no idea what I was supposed to do or what was expected of me. I think I settled on being clean, neat and polite. When actors aren't acting, but are supposed to present themselves as actors, they really are at a loss. I don't think we got the money from Mr. Levine. I do remember afterward drinking a grownup Scotch sour in a cocktail lounge near the East River with Dan, George DiCenzo and a few fellow actors, and talking about how to get "these jerks" to finance "our" film. Dan had the remarkable knack of creating unflagging team loyalty.

Somehow the money was raised, and the fun *really* began. Dan obviously managed to persuade the network powers-that-be at ABC-TV that he could continue to produce a daily half-hour segment of the series while at the same time filming *Dark Shadows*, the movie—with the same cast. Oh, and, by the way, he was going to *direct* the movie. The fact that he had never directed before was easily remedied: for practice, he set about directing several episodes of the soap. I was in the first episode he helmed, with our venerable director, Lela Swift, standing by. I still find it remarkable that the very first television director I ever worked with was a woman. Many years later I realized how much time had passed before I worked with another female director. Lela Swift mother-henned Dan through several more episodes, but there was never really any doubt that he had the makings of a fine director. He was specific, personal and quite a terrifying presence. One's mind did not wander.

The actors were, on the whole, sublimely unaware of the logistics that made this whole unwieldy venture possible. Give actors a script and a call sheet, and they enter a state of oblivion that is blessedly free of any care or concern for anything or anyone else in this universe. We are children. We are stars. We require equal parts discipline and pampering.

I made particular use of my call sheets. I wrote on the backs of them daily throughout the entire grueling, magical 30 days of shooting, beginning with our first day at Lyndhurst. I missed the familiarity and convenience of our own studio, but at the same time savored one of the most joyous experiences an actor can have—shooting on location. What follows are some of my original notes written during the filming of *House of Dark Shadows*.

House of Dark Shadows Journal

1ST DAY OF SHOOTING–MONDAY, MARCH 23, 1970

Ext. Cemetery–Sleepy Hollow Cemetery

Tick, tock—precious little sleep. Up at 4 a.m. and straight into the shower while the coffee perks. Somehow I'm ready to go at 4:45. Thank God I laid everything out last night. It's dark, cold and overcast—perfect cemetery weather. I settle into the back seat of the limousine in dark glasses and curlers. Heck of a way to look in a limo! We pick up Grayson, Sam and Mike Stroka and we're all at Lyndhurst by 6 a.m. Five minutes later we're in makeup chairs—a predawn cheeriness—are we at camp? A kind of cozy conspiracy with our coffee and Danish while superb makeup and hair people go to work. This is their time. I finish first. I hurry to my dressing room, brew tea in my little nest and wait to be called. Finally we're all lumped together in another limo and motor off to the cemetery as though we really are going to a funeral. Are we? Just realized that these fancy limos we were all picked up in this morning are actually going to be used in the funeral scenes. I thought that was too nice a gesture on Dan's part. We'll probably all board a public bus for the trip home tonight.

We're in a 29-acre cemetery and no one can find Dan. He finally turns up, scowling, to set up the first shot. We need rain, but just as we're about to shoot, the skies clear. Thank God for the Tarrytown fire department.

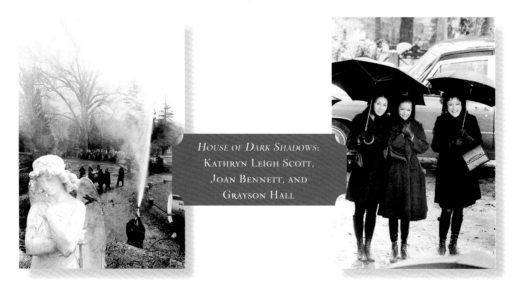

HOUSE OF DARK SHADOWS:
KATHRYN LEIGH SCOTT,
JOAN BENNETT, AND
GRAYSON HALL

The "A" Team is soaked to the skin after the first rehearsal with the fire department hoses. Leave it to Roger Davis to turn and walk away with *our* umbrella before the hoses are turned off. On the next take, *I'll* hold the umbrella. Several false starts and then we go for our first take. Everyone is miserable—and we've only just begun!

On the second take, we get real rain—but Dan says the rain is *slanting*. Now we have to wait until the rain stops so we can let the fire department turn on the hoses and make movie rain.

During the break, I overhear the camera crew talking. One of them says Dan has a great way of bringing unity to the set—everyone hates him. And this is the first day?

On the third take, Dan cuts two lines from the 23rd Psalm. The Assistant Director mutters, "Great. Now he's editing God."

Ten setups later, Dan decides to shoot the POV of the casket just for the hell of it. The assistant director says, "No wonder by lunch we're already three days behind."

We have to pause while a real family arrives to retrieve a real casket stored in the nearby vault. We all try not to stare. They somehow manage to look a good deal more cheerful than we do. I've almost forgotten who's supposed to be in our casket. I'll have to check the script.

We break for lunch. Chicken chow mien from the honey wagon eaten in a school bus, then it's back to misery. Someone's given Thayer David a snort of brandy to ward off the cold and Dan is livid. Who knew? One blast from

THAYER DAVID IN VAMPIRE MODE AND ROGER DAVIS.

Tarrytown's finest and we're all drenched again. Finish two hours late. Johnny Karlen does his "drunken discovery" in the mausoleum and we all hug and applaud him. He's really great! Everyone races to peel off wet clothes. The worst is over all on the first day. [George] DiCenzo says it's all going to be hell, but one fun hell. No pampering—"slop through and don't whine," he advises. The assistant director wonders if anyone asked Dan why he chose these scenes for the first day. Who cares now? I bring home a bouquet of red carnations and white pompoms from the funeral scene. We ride home in regular sedans, of course. Well, we've had our first day. It can be done. I can do it.

KATHRYN WITH JONATHAN FRID IN THE SUN AND JOHN KARLEN IN THE DARK.

2ND DAY OF SHOOTING - TUESDAY, MARCH 24, 1970

Ext. Greenhouse and Stable

Jonathan, young David and I drive out at noon in the station wagon with several sheets of Plexiglas for the prop department wobbling on the roof. Heavy traffic the whole way. With the postal strike, the National Guard is delivering mail—verrry slowly. A cold, icy clear day with the crew bundled in North Pole gear filming Thayer and Roger down by the water. Jonathan and I arrive at the honey wagon for lunch and makeup. Roger is angry about his wardrobe and Thayer complains about the food, but both seem pleased with their scene. It was a good fight they say. Lots of grunting and much blood. Alex is on hand for the stunt work—I catch him draining blood from a leg wound he has self-doctored! Great. Back to lunch. We wait and wait. I'm bored. I ask Jonathan if I should lighten my hair. He says sure. I go ahead and do it with a bottle of peroxide in the basement sink, with the hairdresser looking on. She finds a bottle of Joy dish-washing liquid to use as shampoo. We think my hair looks great, then wonder what Dan will say.

Well, we won't know today because it's a wrap. We're released at five o'clock. Much ado about nothing. Jonathan and I are annoyed and irritable—nothing worse than sitting around—we were both psyched to do our scene. I like my hair color and at least I've had time to coordinate the costumes with the wardrobe dept. Bed by 9:30.

3rd Day of Shooting–Wednesday, March 25, 1970

Ext. Stable and Estate Grounds

Up at 5 a.m. Picked up at 5:45. Jonathan not ready yet, so off we go to get Grayson and Sam. Brisk, early Spring weather. I'm wide-awake and exhilarated. Makeup, hair, wardrobe all accomplished in 45 minutes. I trot out to the meadow in my woolly hat, sweater, scarf and miniskirt. Country casual and sexy--the perfect outfit for meeting your vampire lover. Dan already at work. We walk through the scene together until Jonathan arrives. Timoe is short even though we're the first shot of the day. Everything is done in the first master shot, with the two of us slowly ambling the equivalent of two city blocks. Everything is great, except our hand-clasp and hug is lost behind a branch. We do several close-ups and an extreme close-up hug—then it's over. Done. I'm disappointed. It's freezing cold and I should be glad we got the shot, but I feel I could have done better.

They move on to the Julia and Barnabas walk. I go find Johnny Karlen and we sit chatting, drinking coffee on the grassy hill. Next up—the stable scene. There's an irritating delay as the camera is specially rigged. Johnny and

Dan Curtis

I rehearse during the set up and then relax in the stable yard. I'm called to action and pick up my flashlight for the scene. Again, entire scene is shot in master. It's close, tight work, but we're keyed up for it and aware we've only got 90 minutes to shoot the whole complicated sequence. Mr. Louis "Moviestar" Edmonds wants to know why he isn't on camera more and when his close-up will be done. He insists on another take and now we're down to 15 minutes for Johnny's and my two-shot. Dan can read me like a book and gives me a hug. Don't worry, he says. We do the scene. Two takes and Johnny and I have it. Dan says "Good work! and I know it. I'm finally pleased with something I've done. But it's only because of Johnny. Why can't I always work with

Johnny? He always plays a scene full out with lots of surprises to keep you on your toes. Just as we wrap, someone tells Dan the rushes of the fight scene with Thayer and Roger are really bad, have to be redone. Johnny and I look at each other and scramble out of the stable fast.

Home to bed. It's been a good day's work.

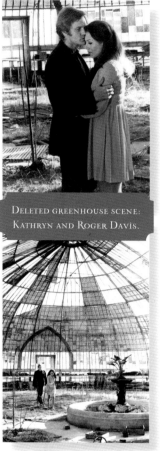

DELETED GREENHOUSE SCENE:
KATHRYN AND ROGER DAVIS.

4TH DAY OF SHOOTING–THURSDAY, MARCH 26, 1970

Int. Collinwood Stable—Bite scenes

6 a.m. call. Hurry up and wait. Cold and cloudy, but as I arrive the sun breaks through. I'm sent back to my dressing room so the fine weather can be utilized for an outdoor scene. I rap with Alex about stunt work. "I use physics," he tells me. "I study the skull. It weighs 16 pounds and it can shift the whole body in a high-speed fall. I toss cats in the air to watch how they twist and turn to break a fall. I go for the money on each take. I'd drive a car up a tree if Dan wanted me to. He's the greatest." Actually, Alex is pretty great himself.

Grayson, Joan, Lisa, Louis and a cast of thousands arrive out of nowhere, all complaining, all waiting for something, *anything*, to happen. A slight drizzle and the crew breaks. Three times I dress and undress and wait some more. Nancy does her semi-nude scene as a vampire. She's the only one who ends up working. No bite scenes today.

5TH DAY OF SHOOTING–FRIDAY, MARCH 27, 1970

Ext. Pool and Greenhouse

Dan's wearing a hard hat. We're not. Hmmmm. The greenhouse is in ruins— and fabulous. Very romantic. Why do I have to wear these silly, skimpy dresses?

6TH DAY OF SHOOTING–MONDAY, MARCH 30, 1970

Ext. Collinwood Stable

Who knows what scenes we'll do, if any. A blizzard has dropped two feet of Easter Sunday snow and it's white Christmas rather than blossom-budding

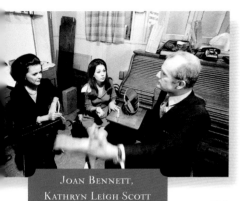

JOAN BENNETT,
KATHRYN LEIGH SCOTT
AND LOUIS EDMONDS.

spring. Exteriors are scrapped. Nancy, Louis, Roger and I are called to do a totally revised scene. I arrive, but I'm the only one. Louis has missed the call, snowbound in the country. Dan is livid and everyone becomes a target. Dennis Patrick stands in for Louis in the scene which is now totally rewritten. Roger screws around with the blocking and the lines, sending Dan around the bend. I want to cry. We have to pause when Louis is supposed to speak. His lines and close-ups will be shot later. Thank God it's over. Joan and I agree life would be perfect without Roger Davis. I change and do a scene with Daphne on the stairway. A small group of us gather in Nancy's dressing room. The assistant director does fabulous mimicry of Louis and Roger.

7TH DAY OF SHOOTING–TUESDAY, MARCH 31, 1970

Int. Staircase/Hallway

It's cold and snowing heavily. Joan and I are in makeup chairs. A plumber arrives to fix a basin. He sees the lips-that-made-the-'30s-famous and asks, Aren't you Joan Bennett." I used to be, she says.

11TH DAY OF SHOOTING - MONDAY, APRIL 6, 1970

Int. Foyer/Library

Another early call. I'm being sewn into my costume, my hair still in curlers when I'm called to the set. Louis, Roger and Jonathan are even less prepared than me to shoot this scene. We fumble and bumble, but Dan calls for a take. I can't believe it—he prints the take even though I still have clips in my hair and pins in my dress! Dan is abrupt and ornery. He just wants film in the can. I'm looking forward to my scene with Barnabas in the library, but also dreading it. It's such a lovely scene and I fear it's going to be rushed. After the master and Jonathan's close-up, Dan finds me in the dining room preparing for the reverse shots. He asks me if it would bother me to wait an hour or so before finishing my close-up so he can shoot

a portion of Nancy's scene. She's been sent off to get into vampire makeup and isn't one bit happy about it. I tell Dan I'm fine about waiting, but I'm terribly disappointed. So is Nancy. How can he shoot that much more in the hours remaining? All of our scenes will be spoiled. I could cry.

15th Day of Shooting - Friday, April 10, 1970

Int. Corridor and Maggie's Room

I have to be in makeup at 6 a.m. I arrive and Joan is already in the makeup chair. I grab a piece of Danish and race upstairs to walk through my scenes by myself with no one else around so I can establish an emotional sequence for myself. We'll start at the end of the scene, of course, and work back to the beginning because of the makeup. I head back downstairs from makeup, feeling pretty confident I can sustain the emotional flow.

Well, I just haven't got the hang of this yet. I produce real tears on six takes, but there are camera problems and the only good take is the one I'm unhappy with. I know my close-up was awful. Bill Gerrity talks to me during lunch. "Save your best for the close-ups," he tells me. "Be selfish. Be smart. Learn to gauge when you can count on a take and don't squander your resources on a rehearsal." He's right. This is a lot different than taping the show every afternoon. I know how to gauge myself for that.

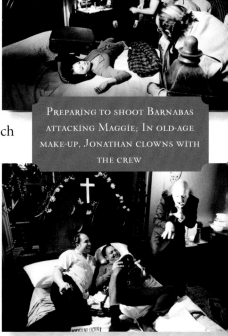

PREPARING TO SHOOT BARNABAS ATTACKING MAGGIE; IN OLD-AGE MAKE-UP, JONATHAN CLOWNS WITH THE CREW

During the afternoon we shoot a sequence with Humbert Astredo playing the doctor and Jeff at my bedside after the bite. Roger waits until the take to scrunch my face up and rest his arm on my nose. I felt like biting his hand, but that would mean rewriting the entire script!

Once again it's a wrap for the day and I leave wondering what I did and if it was any good.

16TH DAY OF SHOOTING—MONDAY, APRIL 13TH, 1970

Int. Julia's Room/Maggie's Room

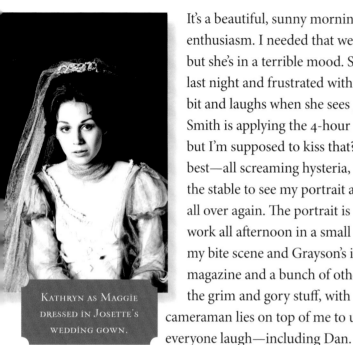

KATHRYN AS MAGGIE
DRESSED IN JOSETTE'S
WEDDING GOWN.

It's a beautiful, sunny morning—and I wake up sunny and full of enthusiasm. I needed that weekend. Joan and I drive out together, but she's in a terrible mood. She's angry she was given her call late last night and frustrated with the daily confusion. She warms up a bit and laughs when she sees Jonathan in the makeup chair. Dick Smith is applying the 4-hour old-age makeup. It looks fantastic— but I'm supposed to kiss that? It's the kind of morning I like best—all screaming hysteria, death and horror. At lunch I go to the stable to see my portrait and feel like screaming hysterically all over again. The portrait is ghastly. Terribly unflattering. We work all afternoon in a small airless room and go overtime doing my bite scene and Grayson's interminable death sequence. *Look* magazine and a bunch of other photographers are on hand for the grim and gory stuff, with Dick Smith the star attraction. The cameraman lies on top of me to use his hand-held camera, making everyone laugh—including Dan.

28TH DAY OF SHOOTING—WEDNESDAY, APRIL 29TH, 1970

Abandoned Monastery/ Rotunda

Lucky me. I get to ride out to Lyndhurst with Roger talking all the way. It's like being with a crowd. Today we begin the long wedding and death sequence. With Dan dropping pages and changing scenes from moment to moment, I'm glad I'm essentially in a trance and have no lines to speak. My wedding dress is a great disappointment to everyone, including me, but we tuck and snip trying to improve it.

29TH DAY OF SHOOTING—MONDAY, APRIL 30TH, 1970

Abandoned Monastery/ Rotunda

5:40 comes damn fast. We worked late and got forced calls this morning. I stumbled out of bed and thought, "Is this any way for a girl to look on her wedding day?" A stake in the heart can't come too soon. I slept in the car and arrived in a misty cold fog—and that was just my mood. It's going to be a tough day. Roger, Jonathan, Johnny and I are working in every shot throughout the sequence. We enter the domed rotunda and are again astonished by the beauty of the set—it's just as we left it last night. It's eerie. Billowing clouds of dry ice and fog machines transform the huge hall into a place quite foreign and magical. Johnny and Jonathan have the worst of the day with special effects. I only have a rather nasty neck bite, ho hum. I walk down the staircase to Barnabas and then spend much of the day on my bed of purple velvet. Roger is impossible. He attempts to direct the scene, but Dan is having none of it. Yet he's invited Roger to come back on the show to play my boyfriend. Why am I being punished? With this news, I develop a craving for cookies. Dwight, the 2nd AD smuggles me coffee, Danish and a bag of Pepperidge Farm cookies which I hide amid the pillows and purple draperies. I'll be Roger's *very fat* girlfriend Maggie.

JOHN KARLEN, ROGER DAVIS AND KATHRYN LEIGH SCOTT.

We return from lunch and find that the school kids have surrounded the house. All afternoon we sign autographs on the balcony. Johnny Karlen is terribly funny—and half-drunk from the vodka Peter slipped him to endure the blood, fog and cobwebs. "Why do I look this way?" he says to the kids. "Because Ol' Barnabas sleeps all day in his coffin while I clean this place and prepare for his wedding. See all those candles in there? Who do you think lit them? Me, that's who—and this is the second dump he's moved into that I had to clean. Sure, I'd like a nice clean cape

KATHRYN AS MAGGIE DRESSED IN JOSETTE'S WEDDING GOWN.

and an elegant velvet smoking jacket, but I gotta rake leaves out of his living room and dust the cobwebs while he sleeps all day—and you know what? Now I catch him sucking blood. What do you think of that?" Johnny had the kids and the entire crew howling with laughter. Then he did a drunken Mussolini on the balcony, exhorting the crowds to give him one last chance. He's lovable, talented and downright nuts. I had pancakes for supper. I'm fattening myself up for Roger.

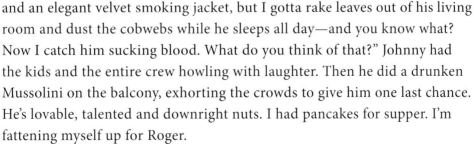

30TH DAY OF SHOOTING—FRIDAY, MAY 1ST, 1970

Abandoned Monastery/ Rotunda

Tick-tock, the clock runs out. There's an ominous feeling on the set as we arrive. The cameras are ready to roll, the scene is rehearsed, but we're hours from shooting. The fans have already gathered outside and it's barely dawn. I go into makeup. It's bites and gore time for all of us. The makeup men get into a tiff among themselves, which means the actors are only half-ready when Dan wants us. I grab a bacon and egg sandwich to hide in the velvet

draperies and run. To hell with the makeup. The wardrobe people have car trouble and arrive late. Ramse Mostoller and Dan go at it and that's the last we see of her for the day. I hop up on my funeral pallet and eat my egg sandwich. Dan calls for rehearsal and I lie down. I promptly fall asleep. Today is the day the film earns its "R" rating. It's just as well I sleep through the blood and gore— blood bladders exploding, stakes in the back and chest, and blood gushing from everyone's mouths. It's ghastly. I try to keep my eyes shut. The special effects men move quickly, skillfully rigging the cross-bow and stakes. The entire morning is spent filming the death sequence of Barnabas and Willie. After one truly grisly take, Johnny calls out "Jonathan, you gotta control your Waterpik!" I notice Jonathan has blood dripping from his nose before the next take—what some method actors will do for their craft! I ask, "Jonathan, are you able to bleed at will like some actors cry at will?" He started to laugh, but then realized it was his own blood—he'd cut himself.

FANS GATHER OUTSIDE THE LOCKWOOD-MATHEWS ESTATE DURING FILMING OF THE FINAL SCENES.

What a wonderful end to a grueling shoot—I rode home with Johnny and Jonathan, my two favorite actors. All of us exhausted but exhilarated. It's a wrap. How in the world will this all come together as a movie? We'll wait and see.

Rehearsing the finale with Dan Curtis, Jonathan Frid, Roger Davis, John Karlen and Kathryn Leigh Scott.

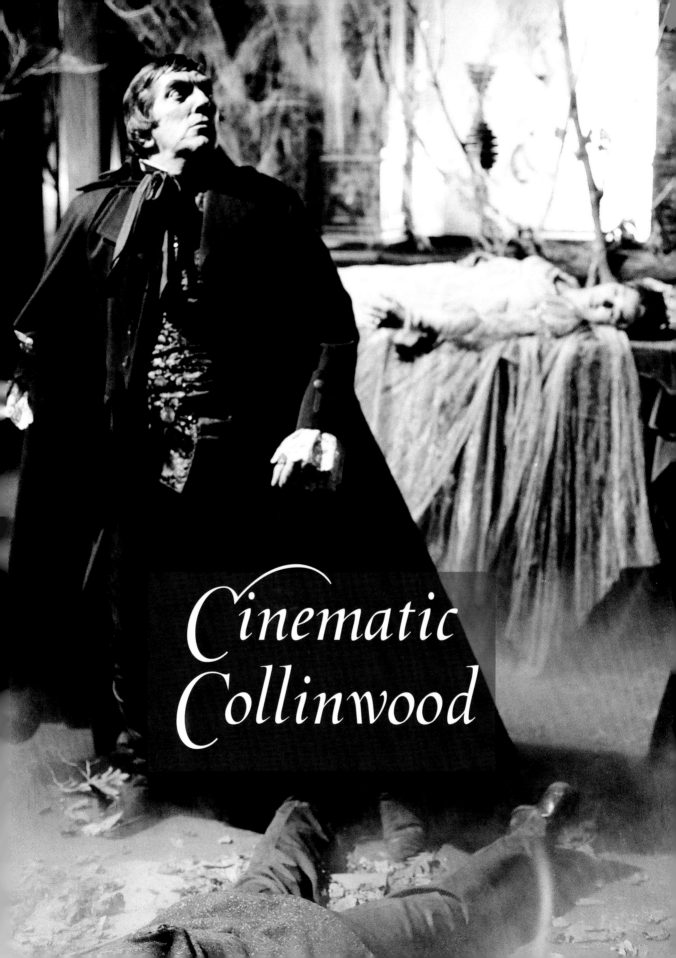

Cinematic Collinwood

HOUSE OF DARK SHADOWS:
JONATHAN FRID AS BARNABAS COLLINS.

By

DARREN GROSS

*I*N LATE 1969, METRO-GOLDWYN-MAYER'S STUDIO CHIEF JAMES AUBREY GREEN-LIGHTED A FEATURE FILM BASED ON THE POPULAR ABC-TV AFTERNOON DRAMA *DARK SHADOWS*. SERIES CREATOR AND EXECUTIVE PRODUCER Dan Curtis had spent nearly a year trying to sell the idea and had been turned down by numerous studios, both large and small. Doubters had been wary of the unusual project and balked at Curtis' insistence on utilizing the TV series cast in a theatrical feature film. *Dark Shadows* was a tremendous television hit at the time, but success on the small screen did not necessarily guarantee a huge motion picture audience. There had been other television spin-off films, but a feature version of a daytime soap opera had never been attempted.

Curtis' idea was to adapt the television series' storyline that introduced vampire Barnabas Collins, played by Jonathan Frid. The television plot originally called for the vampire to be killed off after a few weeks but when Barnabas became so popular with viewers Curtis decided to keep him as a continuing character.

The series' writers took a cue from Frid's characterization of the guilt-ridden vampire, bringing more sympathy to the role. However, Curtis decided that in the film version Barnabas would return to his intended roots as a bloodthirsty monster. Although the sympathetic side of the vampire emerges as the film progresses, the dark side of Barnabas is predominant.

For the screenplay, Curtis turned to series writers Sam Hall and Gordon Russell. Members of the original cast would also appear in the film, reprising their roles. One exception was Clarice Blackburn, who played Collinwood housekeeper Mrs. Johnson on the series. She was tied up working on the soap opera

The Secret Storm, so stage actress Barbara Cason—recently wed to *Dark Shadows* actor Dennis Patrick—stepped into the role for the film.

During the six-week period that *House of Dark Shadows* was being filmed, the television show focused on the 1970 Parallel Time storyline, an alternate universe scenario featuring new characters (with familiar character names). David Selby, Lara Parker, Chris Pennock and Michael Stroka in particular kept the series going while various plot devices were used to cover the temporary disappearance of the actors appearing in the film. For example, obsessed writer William H. Loomis kept Barnabas chained in his coffin for weeks, freeing actor Jonathan Frid for the duration of filming.

In a 1970 interview, Dan Curtis revealed his ambitious plans for the *Dark Shadows* film: "It's not an eensy, teensy movie," he declared. "It's a small budget film with big production values and I think it will make a fortune." Curtis wanted a motion picture that would stand by itself as well as entertain followers of the television show. Working with film (instead of the cumbersome 2-inch quad video used on the daily series) and being able to do more complex editing allowed Curtis to take a much more visceral approach to the horrific material of the story. Unlike the daily series, which had to soft-pedal its shocks to get by the network TV censors, the movie was allowed to be violent and gory. The Motion Picture Association of America rating system was in its early, more liberal days. The GP rating granted to *House of Dark Shadows* in 1970 would merit a PG-13 or R designation today.

Unfortunately Seaview Terrace, the large Newport, Rhode Island estate that had been used for the exterior shots of the television Collinwood, had become a girl's school. The property was also located several hours from the Manhattan studio where the television series was taped, which would have been too great a distance to shuttle actors between the film location and the ABC-TV studio.

In searching for a more convenient filming location, Curtis struck gold with the historic estate known as Lyndhurst, which included a stable area used briefly for filmed location segments of the television show back in 1966. Formerly the home of railroad magnate Jay Gould, the property featured a brooding Gothic manor and 67 acres of land. Only an hour drive from Manhattan, Lyndhurst could be rented for the meager sum of $35,000 at the time. Richard Shore, ASC, cinematographer for the follow-up movie, 1971's *Night of Dark Shadows*, recalls: "The location was amazing. You could never build sets like that for anywhere near

The Lyndhurst estate, gallery, dining room and main hallway.

$35,000." But one condition made by Lyndhurst, a National Historic Trust site, was that tours of the property would continue as scheduled. While the company filmed in one section of the house, tours of the other rooms and the rest of the grounds continued.

For five weeks, Lyndhurst would be home to over 50 actors and crew-members, all of them working to bring *Dark Shadows* to the silver screen. In addition to the castle-like mansion, the grounds included a massive, weather-worn greenhouse, stables, several cottages, a private bowling alley building and a severely decayed pool house. Additionally, sets were built and existing structures were redressed: the kitchen became Julia's laboratory, the stables became Willie's living quarters and nearly every building on the property was shown on-screen in some fashion. The mansion's souvenir shop became the makeup room, the basement was used for wardrobe and the stables became a cafeteria. After each day of shooting, the exposed film was sent to a New York City lab, processed and shown to Curtis the next day in Lyndhurst's makeshift dailies screening room, which was set up in the stables.

The shooting schedule for the film was only 30 days—half the time usually spent on a major studio feature of its scope—and the budget was a slim $750,000. On the first day of shooting, the cast and crew met in the kitchen of Lyndhurst where Curtis sought to rally his troops. Filming was going to be hectic, he announced, and the only way the movie would be finished properly and on time was if everyone pitched in as a team.

Although it was the first feature film for several cast members, most of them took it in stride, remembers Kathryn Leigh Scott, reprising her role of vampire love-interest Maggie Evans. "We'd worked together so long as a close-knit group, isolated in our studio on 53rd Street. Filming on location at Lyndhurst seemed like a natural extension—we'd just taken our show on the road." The handful of cameo appearances made by fellow television show cast members only increased the feeling that the film production was just an extension of the show; Jerry Lacy plays the priest at Carolyn's funeral, Michael Stroka is visible as a pallbearer, Humbert Allen Astredo plays Todd's doctor, Terry Crawford plays a nurse, and Paul Michael plays the old man with the note who awakens Jeff Clark.

The company was blessed with a good omen, remembers associate producer-production designer Trevor Williams. "During the first few days of shooting, one

of the carpenters found a bat on the property. We named it Barnabas and put it in a cage for the rest of the production, feeding it the choicest top sirloin."

On March 23, 1970, shooting began in the vicinity of Lyndhurst in North Tarrytown at the Sleepy Hollow Cemetery—the historic resting place of Washington Irving (author of *The Legend of Sleepy Hollow*) where scenes featuring the Collins mausoleum exteriors and the gloomy funeral of Carolyn (Nancy Barrett) were shot. A false "Collins" nameplate was added to the front of one of the existing structures and then used as the mausoleum. The first sequence shot was the rain-soaked funeral, and instead of a professional Hollywood-style rain machine, Curtis enlisted the Tarrytown fire department, who aimed their hoses into the air off-camera, causing the water to arc back and shower back down onto the assembled cast. "It was the first time I'd been in a film scene with artificial rain," remembers Dennis Patrick, who played Sheriff Patterson in the movie. "We all got completely drenched. After a while, the entire cast was frozen and miserable."

There were some minor disruptions, Williams recalls. "There was a grave-diggers strike going on at the time, so all these bodies to be buried were piling up in one of the buildings where we were shooting. The cemetery hired non-union labor to remove and bury them late in the day. While we were shooting, we kept being interrupted by this procession of workers carrying corpses out. Dan had enough distractions and bellowed, "Can you do that later, please, it's not like they're going anywhere!"

Curtis and crew spent their second day of filming in North Tarrytown, off of DeVries Ave, on the narrow banks of the Pocantico River to film the scenes where a freshly vampirized Stokes attacks Jeff, with stuntman Alex Stevens performing several falls. Both Roger Davis and Thayer David had to wade into the chilly river to film several shots, such as Jeff washing Stokes's blood off of his clothes, and the haunting shot of Stokes's body floating eerily in the river at twilight.

Curtis filmed only nine hours a day, entirely during daylight hours. Night scenes were shot day-for-night, a process whereby night can be replicated on film by using special camera lens filters, altering film exposures, and minimizing the amount of sky shown in exterior shots. Far less time was required to light and set up a shot than they would if the scenes were actually staged at night.

The cast, accustomed to completing an entire television episode each day, filmed an average of 3-6 pages daily, a major adjustment for some of the younger actors.

SHOOTING DAY-FOR-NIGHT WITH
NANCY BARRETT AS CAROLYN STODDARD
RISEN AS A VAMPIRE.

HOUSE OF DARK SHADOWS:
DAN CURTIS DIRECTING WITH
CINEMATOGRAPHER ARTHUR ORNITZ.

"Joan Bennett, again seen as matriarch Elizabeth Collins Stoddard, was used to the rigors of film production, but the rest of us were not as comfortable at first," remembers Kathryn Leigh Scott. "For the series, we were used to rehearsing a script and shooting it straight through, which felt very natural, especially if you've done theater. But for the film, we would shoot pieces of scenes out of sequence, of course."

Curtis had directed some television episodes of *Dark Shadows*, but this was his debut as a film director. During the preparation for *House of Dark Shadows*, he was helped enormously by the series' main director, Lela Swift, who served as his advisor. Despite Curtis' inexperience, he kept the crew on its toes, moving at a brisk pace.

John Karlen, who played Willie Loomis, recalls, "Dan learned very quickly that the actors have to be treated well if they are to successfully bring the characters to life and give the lines meaning. Eventually he became an actor's director. He'd add ideas to your own but never ask you to take things away from your interpretation. He may be harsh or loud with the crew but he'd always be quiet and pleasant with the actors."

Because the house was an historical landmark filled with a wonderful collection of vintage furniture and artifacts, an estate representative was present on the set every day to keep a watchful eye. "We had to be careful of the floors and all of the antiques, but there is no way to shoot on location without causing some nicks and scrapes," says Trevor Williams. "As long as we painted or repaired what we damaged, the estate people were happy." Among the casualties were pieces of antique floor title shattered when filming the scene from *House of Dark Shadows* where Mrs. Johnson discovers Carolyn's body and drops her serving tray.

One of the biggest obstacles during filming was the unpredictable weather. A few days into shooting, the East Coast was hit with a freak spring snowstorm, which put a bit of a damper on things. The cast, scheduled to shoot exterior scenes, showed up on set only to be informed that interior scenes would be filmed instead, scenes for which they were not sufficiently prepared... and some cast members were

DICK SMITH TRANSFORMS JONATHAN FRID INTO A 200-YEAR-OLD BARNABAS AS KATHRYN LEIGH SCOTT DISPLAYS HER VAMPIRE NECK BITE MAKE-UP.

Aged Barnabas bites Maggie.

stranded in Manhattan due to the snowstorm and never got to the set. Joan Bennett remarked, "I never worked on (a film) as hectic as this." For the scene in which the aged Barnabas strangles a cop and attacks Maggie, the casting people had failed to bring in an extra to play the policeman, so Curtis enlisted his longtime production associate George DiCenzo, who also doubled for Jonathan Frid in the scene where Barnabas' silhouette figure is seen approaching Collinwood for the first time.

One of the highlights of the television series was the aging of Barnabas to his true age of nearly 200 years. This impressive effect was created by Dick Smith, the Oscar-winning makeup artist who created the prosthetic appliances for Barnabas' original transformation in 1967. When Barnabas aged in the series, his hair was simply whitened, but for the film Curtis wanted a more horrifying look for Barnabas to accent *House of Dark Shadows'* more villainous interpretation of the vampire. "We decided to make Barnabas bald with a veined, mottled, liver-spotted head, which we basically improvised on the set," remembers Smith. To film the transformation from old Barnabas to his more youthful appearance, the scenes had to be shot out of order. The shots featuring old Barnabas were completed first, ending with Barnabas standing next to Maggie's bed in a fixed position. The camera was then locked down and Frid was taken away to have the aging makeup removed. Then he resumed the scene from the same position while the rest of the segment was filmed. By placing an oil-dissolve effect between the shots, the old Barnabas features melt away into those of the younger Barnabas.

Smith also conjured up makeup appliances for the vampire bites. "I don't want to see the crap you always see," Curtis told Smith. "None of those two stupid little holes. I really want to see that human teeth have really bitten and torn the flesh." Curtis referred to the nasty, realistic bites Smith created as "the worst hickeys in the world."

"I remember bringing quarts of fake blood to the set," says DiCenzo. "Dan really wanted the film to be scary." "When it came to scenes of violence or supernatural shocks, it could never be too intense as far as Dan was concerned," remembers *Night of Dark Shadows* D.P. Richard Shore.

The last *House of Dark Shadows* scene filmed at Lyndhurst was the elaborately staged staking of Carolyn in the stable, which took two days. "We probably shot more takes of Professor Stokes hammering the stake than any shot in the entire film," recalls DiCenzo. "Thayer David wouldn't hit the stake hard enough.

HOUSE OF DARK SHADOWS: KATHRYN LEIGH SCOTT (MAGGIE), LOUIS EDMONDS (ROGER COLLINS) AND JOAN BENNETT (ELIZABETH COLLINS STODDARD) IN DELETED SCENE.

Curtis kept saying, 'Will you stop mincing around and hit the damn thing!' It took about ten takes."

The production then moved to neighboring Scarborough, New York for scenes featuring the Old House, Barnabas' home. While the Old House used in the television series had actually been adjacent to the Lyndhurst estate, it had burned down in the intervening years, so a different location had to be found. The nearby Schoales Estate (also known as Beechwood), with its grand moody presence and square exterior columns was an ideal substitute. Production then moved to Wilton, Connecticut for one day of shooting at the Three Bears Inn, an old, local restaurant. Carolyn's encounter with Willie and Todd's discussion of the vampire attacks with a deputy was filmed there as well as Barnabas and Maggie's date. The outside also doubled as a Collinsport Street for a scene where Willie warns Professor Stokes about Barnabas, but this sequence was deleted from the final cut.

The final days of filming *House of Dark Shadows* took place at the Lockwood-Mathews mansion in Norwalk, Connecticut. The gloomy but decorative old manor was in a state of disrepair at the time, but its combination of grandeur and decay made it an ideal location. It became the abandoned monastery on the fictional St. Eustace Island used for the finale, where Barnabas intends to marry Maggie. Also shot at Lockwood-Mathews were scenes meant to be in the Old House: the room

David locks Maggie in at the beginning of the film, Josette's bedroom, the room Julia uses to prepare Barnabas's injection and scenes in the Old House basement were also filmed there. With clever set-dressing, part of the lower level of the mansion was also used as the interior of the Collins crypt, for scenes where Willie finds Barnabas's coffin, Todd is bitten by vampire Carolyn, and a cut scene where the sheriff, Roger and Stokes find Carolyn's coffin empty.

Trevor Williams accented the natural decay of Lockwood-Mathews with some extra touches—a suit of armor, a cannon, candelabra, yards of fake cobwebs, leaves and fog. "Then we added those huge, gnarled tree branches," remembers Williams. "The idea was that the place had become so decrepit that trees were sprouting through the floor. The balcony surrounding the rotunda was marvelous. It was perfect for shooting from these really high angles down onto Barnabas and the coffins at the bottom."

"I had to lie on that cold floor for hours, pretending to be dead," recalls John Karlen. "The smoke from the fog machine smelled so foul, I began to think it was toxic. I thought that if they didn't let me up soon, I wouldn't have to *pretend* to be a corpse."

At the other filming sites, the production had been relatively free from disturbances but when shooting starting at Lockwood-Mathews, things changed dramatically. The estate was visible from a main road as well as the Connecticut Turnpike, so after a local paper announced the movie was in residence, the company was besieged by mobs of fans hoping to get a glimpse of the actors. "We hadn't been at the other locations long enough for crowds to build," says Kathryn Leigh Scott. "Lyndhurst was far off the road and there was a charge to view the grounds, which most kids probably didn't have the money to pay. But at Norwalk, they could just cross the street and see us. There must have been hundreds of them."

On May 1, 1970, after six grueling weeks, the first *Dark Shadows* movie completed principal photography. While the actors went back to taping the television show, Curtis and film editor Arline Garson began to cut the hours and hours of raw footage into a cohesive form. In order to deliver a flashy, relentless, slam-bang film, Curtis deleted several scenes and shortened many others. Reportedly after a test screening, a controversial sequence was dropped entirely—in this scene young David Collins is found hanged in Maggie's closet, a noose around his neck-a prank David plays on her in the opening scenes of the movie. "The audience at the screening was quite astonished by the amount of violence in the film," remembers Kathryn Leigh Scott. Jonathan Frid, who has always favored subtlety, was not pleased with the gory, relentless nature of the film, and voiced his displeasure in press interviews at the time. "It was one sledge-hammer scene after another." Ironically, the success of the film seems to have had a negative effect on the long-running television series. After parents saw the more bloody and violent *House of Dark Shadows*, some over-reacted by forbidding their children to watch the television episodes, apparently fearing the ABC-TV daytime presentation was equally horrific. In fact, some ABC affiliates began to drop the soap opera around this time and the impact of *House of Dark Shadows* has been attributed as a motivating factor.

To score *House of Dark Shadows*, Curtis turned to Robert Cobert, who had written the music for the series and other Curtis projects. "I wanted to write original music for the film," states Cobert. "But Dan wanted to recycle the television show music. I fought him tooth and nail on that decision but ultimately lost. While the budget was part of Dan's concern, I sincerely feel that he wanted to use the existing music because the fans liked it and Dan thought they would enjoy hearing it in the film."

In 1968, Cobert had composed Curtis' ABC-TV production of *The Strange Case of Dr. Jekyll & Mr. Hyde*, starring Jack Palance. The music was recorded with a 50-piece orchestra and featured rich, vibrant sound and great dramatic intensity. Most of the selections were later re-recorded with a smaller orchestra for use on the *Dark Shadows* daytime show. However, for *House of Dark Shadows*, Curtis used the original, more sumptuous *Jekyll & Hyde* recordings. Because those cues had been written to match specific *Jekyll & Hyde* scenes, some editing had to be done to make the music work for *House of Dark Shadows'* on-screen action- cues would be extended by repeating a phrase or pattern of notes, or a long music cue

HOUSE OF DARK SHADOWS COSTUME PARTY:
ELIZABETH COLLINS STODDARD (JOAN BENNETT),
CAROLYN STODDARD (NANCY BARRETT),
BARNABAS (JONATHAN) AND MAGGIE (KATHRYN),
JEFF CLARK (ROGER DAVIS).

would end abruptly, a stinger (or curtain) added to the end, in an effort to make it work for a shorter scene. This is why some of the music cues are slightly mistimed or edited a bit harshly in the movie's final mix.

Additionally, the *Dark Shadows* television theme was used for the film's main title but a bolder variant with additional reverb, and much more accented chimes and throbbing strings than was used in the series. Robert Cobert did get to compose a couple of original pieces for the film—an easy listening suite of some of the series' themes for use in the party scene and dinner music for Barnabas and Maggie. Cobert originally had a cameo in the party scene as well, playing the piano, but was deleted during editing.

At the last minute, MGM decided that the film needed a name that set it apart from the television show. The film had been produced and filmed as simply *Dark Shadows*. The marketing department came up with *House of Dark Shadows*. The movie's title artwork was then created and used on the trailer, television spots, poster art and print advertising. The title change appears to have been a last-minute alteration of the on-screen title card itself; while all of the promotional materials have the entire title in a uniform, spooky type font, the on-screen title has *House of* in a plain-type font, as if it was added to the existing finished artwork at the very last minute, without the time needed to re-design and re-shoot the entire title card. Most of the advance promotional materials (released to the press during filming) and the resulting news stories referred to the film simply under its shooting title of *Dark Shadows*.

Released in September and October of 1970, *House of Dark Shadows* was an immediate hit, despite overwhelmingly negative reviews. MGM was delighted as they had risked very little on the film and badly needed a hit in a lean period for the studio. Jonathan Frid, Joan Bennett, Grayson Hall, Nancy Barrett and Kathryn Leigh Scott provided promotion in broadcast and print interviews. After three months, *House of Dark Shadows'* net rentals (not grosses which is the current way of noting box office receipts) earned MGM $1,836,000 in the U.S. and Canada. It was also dubbed and released in many different foreign countries, the title translated literally or modified for maximum marketing value.

The success of *House of Dark Shadows* prompted MGM to sign Dan Curtis to a three-picture deal though only one additional film between Curtis and MGM would ever be made. With a working title of *Dark Shadows II* and later changed to *Curse of Dark Shadows*, the second *Dark Shadows* movie would also undergo a last-minute title change, being renamed *Night of Dark Shadows* by the time it was released in the fall of 1971.

Curtis originally intended to resurrect the character of Barnabas for the second film but Jonathan Frid had been unhappy with the bloody, violent aspects of *House of Dark Shadows* and declined to play the role again. This decision coincided with creating a new, human character for Frid (Bramwell Collins) in the final months of the television series.

Rather than recast Barnabas for the next movie, Curtis and Sam Hall came up with an entirely different approach, implementing a creepy mixture of *The Haunted Palace*, *Rebecca* and the 1970 Parallel Time story featured on the *Dark Shadows* series.

Dan Curtis and Sam Hall hammered out the story in meetings, and Hall alone was tasked to write the treatments and screenplay drafts in a short amount of time. By the time it was filmed, the final script had evolved into a perfectly tuned Gothic in a modern setting, featuring obsessive characters, a brooding, eerie atmosphere and genuine chills. Though given a higher budget ($900,000) than before, Curtis again had only six weeks to shoot. This time around, there was actually time for two full days of rehearsals prior to shooting, and there would be no lost time moving to different locations, as the entire film was to be shot at Lyndhurst. There also would be no distractions or demands on Curtis from the TV series production offices, as the ABC-TV series had just ended its five-year run, the last episode recorded a few days before *Night of Dark Shadows* began filming on March 29, 1971.

Spring arrived early in 1971, so the *Night of Dark Shadows* crew enjoyed a mostly sunny, warm production unlike the wintry *House of Dark Shadows* shoot a year earlier. The cast of the second movie was heavily comprised of series regulars who did not appear in the first film. While David Selby had to be written out of the last few episodes of the television show because of appendicitis, he recovered in time to do the movie. Virginia Vestoff, who had played Samantha Collins in the television series, was supposed to play a character of the same name in *Night of Dark Shadows* but she was appearing on in 1776 on Broadway and was unavailable. Therefore the character's name was changed to Laura and played by Diana Millay, who had played a different Laura Collins character in the television show. Series regular Jerry Lacy was intended to play Reverend Trask but was playing Humphrey Bogart in the movie version of *Play it Again, Sam* and unavailable so

NIGHT OF DARK SHADOWS:
DAVID SELBY AS CHARLES COLLINS AND
LARA PARKER AS ANGELIQUE IN A DELETED SCENE
TO BE INCLUDED IN RESTORED VERSION.

the character was changed to Reverend Strack and Thayer David was called upon to play the role. Michael Stroka was originally slated to play the role of a doomed hippie, who breaks into Collinwood in a rainstorm and is lured upstairs by a glowing light, only to be clawed by the ghost of Angelique and clubbed to death by Gerard. This sequence was meant to open the film, but six days into shooting, Curtis decided it was unnecessary and dropped it from the shooting schedule.

Night of Dark Shadows was Kate Jackson's first film. "It was very exciting. I was young and ready to do anything," remarks Jackson. In one scene, she is thrown into a filthy swimming pool. Jackson laughs such unpleasant experiences off. "All of us in the cast did little things that were scary. The scariest one for me was jumping off a horse, running. You had to keep your concentration so you wouldn't get hurt."

As in *House of Dark Shadows*, Curtis came to the set each day knowing exactly what he was going to shoot and how he was going to accomplish it. "Dan does not spend time on irrelevant details. He knows what's important and what to spend money on and he expects you to do your job," says *Night of Dark Shadows* D.P. Richard Shore. "He gives you a general sense of what he wants so you can bring some of your own creativity to the final result."

"It felt more like a Hollywood production than the first film did," reflects John Karlen, who portrayed writer Alex Jenkins. "It was more professional." Unlike *House of Dark Shadows*, every scene of *Night of Dark Shadows* would be shot within the boundaries of the Lyndhurst estate. Any additional sets needed were built on the grounds, including the cemetery, the scaffolding for the hanging scene, and others. The basement of Collinwood was filmed in a long storage cellar underneath the greenhouse. As in *House of Dark Shadows*, *Night of Dark Shadows* was shot entirely in the day, using day-for-night filming techniques for nocturnal scenes. When shooting inside, sheets of black cloth were again hung outside the windows to make it appear that it was night outside.

The production had to go to unusual means to stage the scene where Claire (Nancy Barrett) shoots Gerard (James Storm) through the window. "The gun Nancy Barrett used was filled with blanks," remembers Shore. "We had to make it look like a bullet went through the window when she fired the gun. We had a crewmember stand near James Storm, just off-camera with a slingshot and a B.B. We then placed a sheet of Plexiglass in front of the window to protect Nancy from the B.B. and the shattering glass. Jim was given a rag soaked in stage blood. When Curtis called action, Nancy fired the gun. At the same time, the crewmember fired

NIGHT OF DARK SHADOWS:
JOHN KARLEN AS ALEX JENKINS AND
KATE JACKSON AS TRACY COLLINS;
DAVID SELBY AS QUENTIN COLLINS;
JAMES STORM AS GERARD STILES.

NIGHT OF DARK SHADOWS: GRAYSON HALL AS
CARLOTTA DRAKE, DAVID SELBY AS QUENTIN
COLLINS AND KATE JACKSON AS TRACY COLLINS.

the slingshot; the B.B. shattered the glass and Jim slapped the bloody rag to his head, making blood run down his face. It worked very effectively."

While the photography on *House of Dark Shadows* managed to be both extremely dark and colorful, Curtis wanted a richer palette for the second film. "Dan wanted the flashbacks to have a different look than the modern sequences," remembers Richard Shore. "I tried to make it a little softer, paler. For shots where Angelique was a ghost, I wrapped cloth around the lens to make the edges of the frame appear hazy and ghostly. The ghost attacks were stylized, using slow motion. The (deleted) Quentin and Angelique pool house make-out scene was supposed to be a dreamy fantasy so we made it wild with colored lights, filters and fog."

Shooting in the dilapidated greenhouse was genuinely dangerous. In one scene, Angelique (Lara Parker) lures Alex inside and causes several pieces of glass to come crashing down. Alex leaps aside, narrowly escaping death. Curtis filmed this without a stunt double. "I was very young back then," says John Karlen, "and full of youthful bravado, so Dan was able to talk me into doing it." Trevor Williams remembers, "The panes were all specially rigged to fall and the A.D. (assistant director) said, 'Okay, I'm going to say '1, 2, 3, now' and when I say 'now', release the glass.' Everybody backed out of the shot and hid, waiting for the cue. The A.D.

Night of Dark Shadows deleted dream sequence with David Selby and Lara Parker.

stupidly popped up again and said, 'Remember, when I say 'now . . .' The crew people, only hearing the word 'now,' released the glass, which came crashing down." Unfortunately, the cameras hadn't been rolling. "The A.D. wasn't hurt but we had to go back and reset the whole thing."

Not all of the scenes that seemed treacherous on paper turned out that way. In one sequence cut from the movie, Gerard's Doberman Pinschers terrify Tracy, backing her into a corner of the stables. "The dog trainer (Captain Art Haggerty-visible on-screen as a bald henchmen in the film's 1810 sequences) showed up with these two dogs that looked absolutely savage," remembers Shore. "Everybody was terrified of them. But when we went to work, the dogs turned out to be extremely friendly and would not growl or bark menacingly. It took forever for the trainer to goad them into looking mean."

The scene of Charles Collins' (David Selby's dual role) horse stomping Strack is quite convincing on film, but would have appeared quite absurd on-set. A crew member retrieved two severed horse legs from a slaughterhouse used for pet food and when the shot was filmed, a prop man stood off camera and poked the horse hooves into Thayer David." In a few shots, a stuntman playing Strack crouches, a few feet from the stomping horse, his arm raised, reacting in terror. Shot with a long lens (which compresses depth, making objects appear close together), it appears as if the horse is near or right on top of the character.

While the production was not hampered by the weather problems encountered on the first film (there was rain on a few days, but cover sets had been designated in case it rained, and were used without too much trouble), Curtis was moving at a slower pace, utilizing long elaborate tracking shots, tricky hand-held camerawork, and cramped rooms, that were tricky to light and film in. While the production was still getting many more setups (between 18 and 25 on average) in the can each day than a typical Hollywood production, doing the script justice was requiring more camera coverage (ie: different camera angles of the same action taken with different lenses and from different vantage points) than anticipated, and eating up time. Adding to the delay was a problem with the film lab. More than half a day's filming was ruined in the lab, all of it requiring hasty re-shoots. Gerard's death scene was originally staged with the character falling from the railroad bridge onto electrified power lines where he is burnt to a crisp. Unfortunately, the Gerard dummies used for the electrocution effect weren't deemed convincing enough when the dailies were screened, so the death was re-shot with Gerard falling to his death on the railroad tracks below.

The exciting car chase scene climaxed somewhat differently than planned. Originally Gerard is supposed to drive Alex's car off of the road so that it tumbles down the embankment and rolls over. Netting was set up off the side of the road to catch the car when it went off the road and out of the shot. Unfortunately, stuntman Alex Stevens, who was driving, turned the wheel too late and instead of going off the road near the trees, plowed right into one full-speed. Assistant cameraman Ron Lautore was in the car, filming with a handheld camera, and when the car hit the tree, the impact caused the eyepiece to collide with his eye-socket. Thankfully he escaped with only a black eye, but Alex Stevens injured his leg as a result. This was par for the course on this stunt-filled production, according to James Storm, "There was a lot of physicality on the film—nearly every stuntman went to the hospital."

Night of Dark Shadows finished production eight days behind schedule on May 18, 1971, and was then edited and scored in New York. Curtis again enlisted Robert Cobert to write the music score, this time allowing him to create a significant amount of original cues as well as recycling some pieces from the television series. The melodies for the film were not written to match specific scenes but were designed to evoke a certain mood. They were recorded in a single day with an orchestra of no more than half-a-dozen players. For the main title and love theme, Cobert reused the somber but lovely *Joanna's Theme* from the television series, utilizing a new version with harmonica. The popular *Quentin's Theme*, which was originally written as a dance hall theme for *The Strange Case of Dr. Jekyll & Mr. Hyde*, was also featured in a variety of styles.

In late July, when *Night of Dark Shadows* was completed, Curtis, Cobert and screenwriter Sam Hall flew to Los Angeles to screen the film at MGM's headquarters in Culver City with executive James Aubrey and his underlings. Much to Curtis' surprise, the studio heads were dissatisfied with the finished film. Writer Sam Hall could tell that the screening was not going well, "The film just seemed to go on and on and on. I started slinking down in my seat more and more as it went on." Aubrey demanded that more than a half hour be eliminated from *Night of Dark Shadows*, ordering a revised cut be delivered the same time the next day—a ridiculously inadequate amount of time in which to properly accomplish such a major alteration. Curtis, film editor Charles Goldsmith, and a team of editors had spent several frantic weeks on what they thought would be their final cut. If Curtis now did not deliver a shorter version overnight, Aubrey threatened that he would have it recut himself, without Curtis's input.

Dan Curtis, Hall & Cobert sat down with the script and started going through it, trying to find sequences they could cut. Aubrey had singled out Grayson Hall, particularly, and Sam Hall fought hard to keep her scenes, but with the amount of footage they had to remove, some of her material was going to have to go. The group was then given an older MGM staff editor who went through the film hurriedly cutting and splicing as Dan instructed. David Selby was quickly flown out to California to record a new voice-over (that plays while Carlotta watches the group approach the house near the climax) in an effort to make the final scenes

NIGHT OF DARK SHADOWS:
THE HANGING OF ANGELIQUE.
BOTTOM LEFT: DAVID SELBY AS
CHARLES COLLINS AND THAYER DAVID AS
REVEREND STRACK FLANK A HANGMAN.

Night of Dark Shadows cast photo shoot:
Grayson Hall, Kate Jackson, Lara Parker, James Storm,
John Karlen, David Selby and Nancy Barrett.

NIGHT OF DARK SHADOWS:
LARA PARKER, KATE JACKSON, GRAYSON HALL
AND NANCY BARRETT.

make sense, now that the climactic séance was removed. Cobert also adjusted his music score to fit the revised edit, dropping a cue and adjusting others in the re-mix. They screened the film the next day, as ordered, now down to a raggedy 97 minutes. Says Curtis "Aubrey got up, and said 'It's a tight little thriller.' I said, 'But it doesn't make any sense!' to which he said 'With your audience, it doesn't matter.' He then walked right out of the screening room."

On the plane back from Los Angeles, Hall broke down and cried about the devastating situation they had just experienced. "It wasn't just my work they butchered, but my wife Grayson's as well. That affected me more. I didn't want to have to tell her," recalls Hall.

Premiering August 4 of 1971, *Night of Dark Shadows* garnered mostly lack-luster reviews, presumably due in part to the heavy editing enforced by MGM that compromised the continuity and clarity of the story. The film, accordingly, did not generate as much revenue as *House of Dark Shadows* but actually wasn't the flop it has since been purported to be. Its three-month U.S. and Canadian net rental receipts brought MGM $1,400,000—quite a respectable sum in 1971.

Naturally, *Dark Shadows* devotees would like to see both *House of Dark Shadows* and *Night of Dark Shadows* extended to include all of the scenes shot but omitted from the released versions. Although none of the deleted footage—referred to in the film business as trims and outs—for *House of Dark Shadows* survives, Dan Curtis' original director's cut of the longer version of *Night of Dark Shadows* was discovered in the Warner Brothers deep storage vaults in 1999. In a fortunate case of corporate synergy, Warner Brothers owns the pre-1986 MGM library of motion pictures, including *House of Dark Shadows* and *Night of Dark Shadows*. With Warner Brothers also releasing the 2012 *Dark Shadows* film star-ring Johnny Depp, the studio has committed to restore *Night of Dark Shadows* so Curtis' unseen original cut can finally be made available, finally lifting the "curse" of Dark Shadows after four decades.

NIGHT OF DARK SHADOWS:
LARA PARKER AS ANGELIQUE AND
DAVID SELBY AS CHARLES COLLINS.

Dark Shadows Reborn

DARK SHADOWS
THE WICKED AND THE DEAD
JERRY LACY AND JOHN KARLEN IN

XV

THE FOOL

THE DEVIL

AN ORIGINAL DRAMATIC READING

DARK SHADOWS
THE NIGHT WHISPERS
AN ORIGINAL AUDIO DRAMA

JONATHAN FRID

JOHN KARLEN

AND

BARBARA STEELE

DARK SHADOWS
BLOOD DANCE
DAVID SELBY AND LISA RICHARDS IN

AN ORIGINAL DRAMATIC READING

DARK SHADOWS
ECHOES OF INSANITY
JOHN KARLEN AND LARA PARKER IN

AN ORIGINAL DRAMATIC READING

KATHRYN LEIGH SCOTT AND DAVID SELBY IN

Dark Shadows

THE BOOK OF TEMPTATION

WITH LARA PARKER, JOHN KARLEN
AND DAPHNE ASHBROOK

STUART MANNING IS ONE OF THE WRITERS AND PRODUCERS
OF THE *DARK SHADOWS* AUDIO DRAMAS. HE MAINTAINS A
DARK SHADOWS BLOG AT
WWW.COLLINWOOD.NET/NEWS.

By
STUART MANNING

THE ABC-TV *DARK SHADOWS* TELEVISION SERIES ENDED PRODUCTION IN 1971, BUT FOR MANY OF ITS FAITHFUL VIEWERS THE IDEA OF REUNITING THE CAST OF CHARACTERS REMAINED A FERVENT DREAM. DESPITE THE proposal of a television reunion movie in the 1980s, an on-screen sequel was not to be. It wasn't until 2003 that Dan Curtis Productions would sanction an official continuation with the original cast. However, this would be a different, fresh format—a brand-new audio drama, similar to a radio play, featuring a dozen of the show's veteran actors picking up their characters' lives more than 30 years later.

Return to Collinwood was first performed live on stage at the 2003 *Dark Shadows* Festival at the Brooklyn Bridge Marriott in New York before being released on compact disc via MPI Home Video. The production, written by Jamison Selby—son of original *Dark Shadows* actor David Selby—was a warm-hearted reunion which paid tribute to the show's characters and performers alike, even answering the long-standing mystery of governess Victoria Winters' heritage. It also established that there was a potential market for new stories in an audio format and, more importantly, a cast of original actors who were willing to participate in the production of new stories.

In 2006, I was part of a proposal by London-based audio producers Big Finish Productions to license *Dark Shadows* for a special project to mark the show's 40th anniversary. Big Finish had a track record of creating high-quality original dramas for the CD market. Having produced hundreds of plays for licensed brands such as *Doctor Who*, we were excited at the chance to tackle an

MARCH 2010 LOS ANGELES RECORDING SESSION
WITH JERRY LACY, LARA PARKER, DAVID SELBY,
KATHRYN LEIGH SCOTT, JAMES STORM, JOHN KARLEN,
JAMISON SELBY AND ANDREW COLLINS.

American property. With an agreement in place, the first batch of new stories was recorded in Los Angeles in May, 2006. *Dark Shadows* was now, truly, reborn.

The House of Despair began a new unfolding serial for the *Dark Shadows* characters. Set several years after the original contemporary storylines of the late 1960s and early 1970s, it began with Quentin Collins returning to Collinsport to reclaim the Collins family homestead and face new supernatural threats. It was a conscious decision to make the new episodes stand apart from *Return to Collinwood*. That story had presented a rare, mostly happy ending for the characters, older and mostly content decades later. Setting the Big Finish stories earlier, we could create our own distinct continuity while filling in some of the mysteries from those lost decades.

That first series of audio stories was released in late 2006. Buoyed by their success, new possibilities for *Dark Shadows* were explored. In 2008, British actor Alec Newman appeared alongside original series actress Kathryn Leigh Scott in two dramatic readings—*Clothes of Sand* and *The Ghost Watcher*. Alec had starred as Barnabas Collins in the *Dark Shadows* 2004 pilot. The first story cast him as the predatory Sandman, a malevolent voice haunting the dreams of a traumatised

Maggie Evans. The play offered Alec a chance to renew his *Dark Shadows* ties and give fans an idea of how his version of Barnabas might have developed.

Although Big Finish had succeeded in recruiting the newest actor to play Barnabas, his original incarnation remained elusive. Jonathan Frid had declined an invitation to appear in the ongoing full-cast dramas, but in 2008 he made it known that he might consider a one-off return to the role he made immortal. Well aware of the weight of expectation involved, Jonathan took some persuasion and had strong instincts about the story. Over a period of months, an outline was developed from his ideas and the project began to gain momentum. Jonathan rightly felt very invested in Barnabas and was keen that any new chapter did the character justice. It took two years to happen, but when he finally went before the microphone in a Toronto studio in April of 2010 to perform *The Night Whispers*, it marked a genuine milestone—the first and only time Jonathan Frid would reprise the role of Barnabas Collins.

As the *Dark Shadows* audio dramas have grown in number, the scope and ambition of the productions have developed in tandem. A secondary range of dramatic readings—stand-alone stories focusing on specific characters—now complements the full-cast releases, which continue to forge separate, ongoing story arcs. The most recent serial, *Kingdom of the Dead*, drew together a cast from all three television versions of *Dark Shadows,* with recording taking place in Los Angeles, New York and London.

Over the years, the production process has become more streamlined and technology has come on in leaps and bounds. A studio session from Los Angeles can now be digitally downloaded by an editor in London within hours, and actors on opposite sides of the Atlantic can be seamlessly combined into a single scene. In some respects, it's a world away from the original *Dark Shadows*, but at its heart it remains very much the same. Technology aside, the emphasis is still on fast turnaround recording, relying on the adrenaline and the skill of the actors. Just like the original show, everyone involved is still painting fantasy worlds with a handful of words while daring the audience to believe.

Dark Shadows has endured because of its characters and that original, brilliant cast of actors. The soap opera format will always be about worlds without end, and with the right stories any character's journey can be infinite. Five decades on, those personalities still burn brightly, and it's a privilege to guide them through new adventures.

2040 LONDON RECORDING SESSION FOR
KINGDOM OF THE DEAD WITH ALEC NEWMAN AND
LYSETTE ANTHONY; JONATHAN FRID RECORDING
THE NIGHT WHISPERS IN TORONTO; JAMES STORM,
JERRY LACY AND JOHN KARLEN REHEARSE IN LOS
ANGELES; TERRY CRAWFORD AND MARIE WALLACE
RECORD *THE DOLL HOUSE* IN NEW YORK;
ALEC NEWMAN AND KATHRYN LEIGH SCOTT
RECORD *THE GHOST WATCHER* IN LONDON.

Dark Shadows

A POEM

Forty some years ago, so far away
but the memories through time do burn
as if they happened only yesterday
and back to Collinwood I do return

When a certain evil ghost did appear
with a spell to cast and a plot to scheme
Luring children to a room so to hear
an old grammophone playing
    Quentin's theme

His frock coat covered a physique so lean
you knew he had to have something mean
    up his sleeve
All his wickedness had yet to be seen
His spirit was such they had to believe

There was no choice but to pack up
    and leave
But Barnabas came to even the score
though ended back where he couldn't
    foresee
Trapped in his coffin, a vampire once more

He travels through time where
    Quentin's alive
Mysteries, secrets and intrigues galore
and son-of-a-gun ratings revive
with millions of fans clamoring for more

Dark Shadows had more surprises of doom
Quentin's zombie who rises and walks
then is a werewolf who howls at full moon
but in day sounds normal now that he talks

Suddenly a cure for his curse is found
which Count Petofi finally effects
Now Quentin's immortal and more
    renowned
but the vampire's taste for beautiful necks

again wrecks havoc with Barnabas' life
When Angelique dies, Barnabas is lost
So is his chance for a beautiful wife
Grief-stricken he knows what this has
    all cost

And with Julia climbs the stairway
    through time
Then Quentin destroys the stairs to the past
But the memories are there, yours and mine
Shadows of the night and the spell they cast.

by David Selby

Acknowledgments

Our deep appreciation to
Colleen Atwood, Tim Burton, Alice Cooper, Christi Dembrowski, Johnny Depp,
Shep Gordon, David Kennedy, Michelle Pfeiffer and.Richard Zanuck,
With special thanks to Sarah Clark, and to everyone
at Warner Brothers, including Jan Craft, Kolette Kleber and Susannah Scott.

With our special thanks to Dennis Baker, Nancy Barrett, Cheryl Carrington,
William Chu, Robert Cobert, Kathleen Cody, Donald Frid, Jonathan Frid, Jean Graham,
Darren Gross, Guy Haines, Ray Isbell, Roy Isbell, Roberta Jacobs-Meadway, Mark Lawrence,
Stuart Manning, Ben Martin, Claire Morales, MPI Home Video, Jay Nass, Lara Parker,
Henry Plimack, Lilo Raymond, Kathleen Resch, Marcy Robin, David Selby,
Jeff Thompson, Sy Tomashoff, Marie Wallace and Ann Wilson.

PLEASE VISIT OUR WEBSITE FOR OTHER BOOKS BY
KATHRYN LEIGH SCOTT AND POMEGRANATE PRESS:
WWW.KATHRYNLEIGHSCOTT.COM